BRIGHT NOTES

SISTER CARRIE BY THEODORE DREISER

Intelligent Education

Nashville, Tennessee

BRIGHT NOTES: Sister Carrie
www.BrightNotes.com

No part of this publication may be used or reproduced in any manner whatsoever without written permission, except in the case of brief quotations in critical articles and reviews. For permissions, contact Influence Publishers http://www.influencepublishers.com.

ISBN: 978-1-645424-80-2 (Paperback)
ISBN: 978-1-645424-81-9 (eBook)

Published in accordance with the U.S. Copyright Office Orphan Works and Mass Digitization report of the register of copyrights, June 2015.

Originally published by Monarch Press.
Charlotte A. Alexander, 1965
2019 Edition published by Influence Publishers.

Interior design by Lapiz Digital Services. Cover Design by Thinkpen Designs.

Printed in the United States of America.

Library of Congress Cataloging-in-Publication Data forthcoming.
Names: Intelligent Education
Title: BRIGHT NOTES: Sister Carrie
Subject: STU004000 STUDY AIDS / Book Notes

CONTENTS

1) Introduction to Theodore Dreiser — 1

2) Summary — 7

3) Textual Analysis
   - Chapters 1–7 — 9
   - Chapters 8–18 — 28
   - Chapters 19–32 — 46
   - Chapters 33–47 — 64

4) Character Analyses — 86

5) Critical Commentary — 94

6) The Accomplishments of Theodore Dreiser — 103

7) Essay Questions and Answers — 113

8) Bibliography and Guide to Further Research — 120

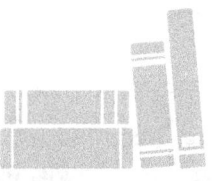

INTRODUCTION TO THEODORE DREISER

BIOGRAPHICAL BACKGROUND

Theodore Dreiser, born in Terre Haute, Indiana in 1871, received his early education in the public schools of the state. He attended Indiana University briefly before embarking on the journalistic career (in Chicago, St. Louis, and Pittsburgh) which would also provide the springboard for his fiction. By the time he became editor-in-chief of Butterick Publications (in 1907) in New York City, his first novel, *Sister Carrie* (1900), had been published. By 1912, when a novel titled *The Financier* was issued, Dreiser had given up newspaper work and devoted himself to fiction. All of his writings, however, from *Sister Carrie* to the popular *An American Tragedy* (1925) to his later works, reflect his Hoosier home life and his early professional experiences. Dreiser was born and brought up in an atmosphere of poverty, rootlessness and religious dogmatism. His father was German, a strict Catholic. He knew what it meant to live on the "wrong side of the tracks," to hunger for material success and pleasure, and to resent the idealistic religiosity of a father who was an economic failure. In fact, he has related the facts and feelings of his life up to age twenty-three in *A Book About Myself*, describing autobiographically, with the same documentary honesty and nonmoralizing frankness he always employed in his fiction, the details of a youthful theft;

his father's increasing loss of initiative and ability to cope with the business world; and his tenderness toward his mother, who represented strength and devotion. As Dreiser puts it, his family seemed in retrospect "of a peculiarly nebulous, emotional, unorganized, and traditionless character." Yet, along with the financial disaster and futility (for even his beloved mother was a poor manager), as well as their being occasionally ostracized by the community for breaking the conventional rules of propriety, there was warmth. Thus much of Dreiser's fiction is peopled with these figures from his family - father, mother, sisters, brothers - as well as filled with remembered past happenings. After living in New York, and traveling, Dreiser ended his days in southern California, dying in 1945.

DREISER'S WORKS

Dreiser's major works are *Sister Carrie* (1900), *Jennie Gerhardt* (1911), *The Financier* (1912), *The Titan* (1914), *The "Genius"* (1915), *An American Tragedy* (1925), *The Bulwark* (1946), and *The Stoic* (1947). In addition, there are invaluable autobiographic writings which form the following chronological sequence: *Dawn* (1931), *Newspaper Days* (1931; first published as *A Book about Myself*, 1922), *A Traveller at Forty* (1913), and *A Hoosier Holiday* (1916). Aside from his journalistic writings, he wrote some essays. It is also worth mentioning that *The Bulwark* and *The Stoic* (issued posthumously) display his later interest in religious philosophy.

THEMES: THE INDIVIDUAL AGAINST UNIVERSAL FORCES

Even in Dreiser's first novel, *Sister Carrie* (1900), it is possible to trace his lifelong preoccupation with people caught up in forces beyond their control, characters who remain to some extent unaware of their conditions and conflicts and who are to a large degree helpless to change the course of their lives. Dreiser writes of a Carrie or a Clyde Griffiths out of a general sympathy toward such human beings (as well as out of a particular sympathy born of his own experiences) - individuals swirling in the complex of a growing, industrialized, mechanized and impersonal America. In 1921, while he was writing *An American Tragedy*, and reflecting back upon his thoughts at the time *Sister Carrie* appeared, Dreiser simply reiterated this **theme** which governed most of his work: "I never can and never want to bring myself to the place where I can ignore the sensitive and seeking individual in his pitiful struggle with nature - with his enormous urges and his pathetic equipment." He emphasized this further (in *The Story of My Life*, 1932), by asserting that "most men and women are haunted by poverty, and all are helpless in the clutch of a relentless fate." However, his views of the possibility of social amelioration were to become somewhat more optimistic between the time of *Sister Carrie* and later works such as *An American Tragedy*.

AUTOBIOGRAPHICAL SOURCES IN DREISER'S WORK

As suggested above, Dreiser's childhood and early adulthood in Indiana was a not uncommon mixture of poverty and puritanical religiosity (in this case, the stern Catholicism of his German father), from which his brothers and sisters in their varying ways rebelled and escaped - the sisters in a manner not unlike the situation of *Sister Carrie*. Dreiser himself first followed the American materialistic dream to Chicago, at fifteen, where he attempted to lift himself out of poverty through a variety of jobs, like dishwashing and selling hardware. In addition, he tried, perhaps, to "find himself" in a year spent at Indiana University.

The road to success he did find, however, was in journalism (his first job with the *Chicago Daily Globe* as reporter led to better ones); and his inclination toward reportorial detail threads throughout his work, especially in the courtroom documentation of *An American Tragedy*, Book III.

Dreiser's temperament and background were well suited to the type of journalism required by the papers he worked for (and eventually, to the fiction he produced). His employers asked for and got from the young journalist vivid, detailed pieces about all the aspects of city life, from social and business levels to the sordid depths of metropolitan poverty and despair. By the time he moved to New York and editorial work in 1894, Dreiser was a successful, skilled reporter, and was in an excellent position to draw upon all his former experiences for the fiction he then began to write - first a cautious series of short stories, the success of which pleased and surprised him, and then *Sister Carrie*. Thus many of the aspects and **episodes** of *Sister Carrie* (as well as his other fiction) can be considered autobiographical, from the Midwestern heroine and her two lovers (associated with exactly similar incidents in the lives of Dreiser's sisters, for example) to the streetcar strike which resembles one covered by the author while he worked for the *Toledo Blade*.

HISTORICAL BACKGROUND: DREISER'S PICTURES OF AMERICA

It is very clear, however, that in addition to the source of autobiography, Dreiser in his writings drew upon his acute awareness of the growing America of his time: his novels provide a carefully detailed, often almost documented picture of his own American society, as he saw it. It is as if he felt the pressure, the responsibility - perhaps because of his many and varied youthful experiences - to expose a new and rather monstrous America which found its gigantic, sprawling expression around 1900 and thereafter. This America was an industrialized, urban society which had developed as rapidly as the huge fortunes (in oil, meatpacking, steel, railroad speculation etc.) which supported it. Unfortunately such rapid transformation of a country was bound to carry with it the extremes of poverty, and Theodore Dreiser was no stranger to the slums of the cities he knew - especially Chicago and New York. What disturbed Dreiser most (and many another observer of the era) was the huge gap between good old American ethics and religious standards still being preached daily, and the actual practices of those who yet listened complacently and comfortably to the preachers. In short, it is the **theme** of hypocrisy which Dreiser took up as a cause in his writing; and it is this hypocrisy - the false front, the appearance of virtue and the practice of ruthless realities - which he undertook to expose in such writings as *Sister Carrie*. Dreiser had come to believe that the society, not its people individually, was corrupt; or rather, he disbelieved that men are born sinful, suggesting (to the discomfort of some of his earlier readers) that hypocrisy, corruption, not to mention sheer poverty, are not conducive to building character or strength of will - the lack of which we see so demonstrated in the structure of Sister Carrie's personality. Such a society is more likely, instead, to produce seduction, adultery, crime, selfishness, waste. And Dreiser saw such results so inevitable as to rule out the possibility of condemning the actors and actresses in his tragedies although the reasons for their decline or ultimate unhappiness are always carefully spelled out.

DREISER'S NON-JUDGMENTAXL ATTITUDES

Dreiser's consistently humane and sympathetic attitude toward his material - his characters, their stories - throughout his writing career should be stressed. No doubt such an attitude is due in part to the lack of prevailing conventional propriety in his own early life, which is just what he claims for Sister Carrie, upon the occasion of her first acceptances of favors from Drouet; there were no strong home traditions to hold her. Dreiser presents the facts of life as he sees them - that is, pragmatically - not as readers especially of his own era) would expect them to be. Such matter-of-fact presentation of the experiences of his characters, however, combined with his indifference toward the **conventions** of reward and punishment, indicate that his attitudes (while born of his own autobiographical background, personally, and nurtured on the hypocritical materialism of his times) deepened into "philosophy": the belief that any ethic, any sense of love or justice, must spring from the individual's actual experience with forces both inside and outside himself combined with his own growing awareness of self (the cultivation of intellect and sensibilities), in order to make judgment - reasoned action - possible, a state which no fully developed characters created by Theodore Dreiser ever reach.

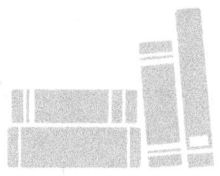

SISTER CARRIE

SUMMARY

....

Dreiser's first picture of human and social conditions, however, reflecting this very indifference toward conventional morality and toward the traditions of reward and punishment - *Sister Carrie* - encountered difficulties of publication, although Doubleday had been formally committed to publish it. Not only that Carrie escaped punishment, but that Dreiser did not look upon her life as sinful, was an insult to late nineteenth century conventionality (expressed, for example, in the horrified response of Mrs. Doubleday to the novel). However, Mrs. Doubleday's horror may have been exaggerated in the tale retold so often as to have become a legend, partly through the interest and friendship of such writers as H. L. Mencken. A young novelist, Frank Norris, as editorial reader for Doubleday, helped in the original acceptance of the novel for publication. Norris' own work would so resemble Dreiser's in its frankness and exposure of the hypocrisies and inequalities of American life that it was inevitable he should heartily applaud this author. Dreiser's publishers issued a minimum number of copies, without advertisement, and the author netted less than a hundred dollars from the novel. A decade or so would have to evolve (during which the author suffered depression and futility at the reception of *Sister Carrie*, and found himself less and less able to attempt more fiction) before the book would receive its proper critical acclaim; in 1907, when the novel was reissued, and thereafter, the public was more receptive to *Sister Carrie*.

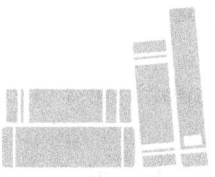

SISTER CARRIE

TEXTUAL ANALYSIS

CHAPTERS 1-7

CHAPTER 1: THE MAGNET ATTRACTING: A WAIF AMID FORCES

From the first paragraph of Theodore Dreiser's *Sister Carrie* the reader learns, importantly, that Caroline Meeber, eighteen years old, is just another poor girl headed for the big city and some kind of new life materially better than the one she is leaving behind. Her satchel is imitation; she brings her own lunch; she carries with her very little money. Furthermore she is "bright, timid, and full of the illusions of ignorance and youth." Her farewell to the flour mill where her father works is easy, rather than regretful.

Dreiser quickly hints of what is to come: "When a girl leaves her home at eighteen, she does one of two things. Either she falls into saving hands and becomes better, or she rapidly assumes the cosmopolitan standard of virtue and becomes worse." But when a country girl leaves home for the city, "there are large forces which allure with all the soulfulness of expression possible in the most cultured human.... Half the undoing of the unsophisticated and natural mind is accomplished by forces wholly superhuman. A blare of sound, a roar of life, a vast array of human hives, appeal to the astonished senses in equivocal terms." Caroline Meeber's story, then, is also to be an account - a damaging one - of social conditions in an American city. It is Chicago, though it could have been New York or any metropolis during the period which Dreiser pinpoints as 1890–1900. The forces which act upon the individual are often described in great detail.

In short, we find out in Chapter One where Caroline comes from, what she may be up against in the big, strange city, what she herself is like, and how she at first responds to people and scenes. That Caroline has been called "Sister Carrie" by her family "half affectionately" is the author's irony. Here he introduces the basis for Carrie's future conflicts: "Self-interest with her was high, but not strong. It was, nevertheless, her guiding characteristic...she was a fair example of the middle American class-two generations removed from the emigrant." At this point, as readers, we plunge with Dreiser's "half-equipped little knight" and her "wild dreams of some vague, far-off supremacy," into the initial dialogues of the novel.

Introducing Charles Drouet, the author takes trouble to define him in terminology of the 1900s as a "drummer" and a "masher." (To the twentieth century reader he is quickly typed as the "traveling salesman.") Carrie's inner conflict is again emphasized, a conflict which Dreiser masterfully describes in the opening passages of Chapter Eight: "In Carrie - as in how many of our worldlings do they not? - instinct and reason, desire and understanding, were at war for the mastery. She followed whither her craving led." As Drouet, recognizing her naivete at once, makes his experienced pitch, Carrie is confused by a mingling of "the instincts of self-protection and coquetry." But Drouet has developed both a manner and a method, and has doubtless pursued them through in the past to numerous successes. Drouet's manner is first of all suggested by his carefully chosen clothes, which, described in detail, are designed to attract women. In his essentially physical nature, he is a nonmoral pleasure-seeking man - in short, a "masher." His method is one of directness, daring, familiarity: he will touch a woman with ease, wait upon her, address her unhesitatingly by her first name - " ... and from then on, by dint of compliment gently insinuated, personal narrative, exaggeration and service, he would win her tolerance, and, mayhap regard."

The remainder of Chapter One is devoted to Drouet's finding "a clue to her interest" and to Carrie's responses. The first clue is "clothes" - her awareness of his impressive appearance and of her own shabby apparel; her associations of longing for the contents of the shopwindows of those businessmen whom Drouet claims to know in her home town. At the same time, as they converse more and more easily, Carrie is reminded by "a little ache in her fancy" of the contrast between the promise of "material prospect" Drouet presents, and her own prospect of day-to-day drudgery in the job she hopes to find in Chicago. "There was much more passing now than the mere words indicated. He recognized the indescribable thing that made up for fascination and beauty in her. She realized that she was of interest to him from the one standpoint which a woman both delights in and fears." When this typical, universal cat-and-mouse game between them is at least temporarily resolved by their exchange of addresses, Carrie is deeply impressed by the roll of greenbacks Drouet produces from his pocket: thus the **theme** of an almost materialistic monomania, born of material deprivation, is established by Dreiser.

To close Chapter One, and to remind the reader of the importance of the city in this novel, Dreiser captures rather dramatically its atmosphere, the mood of its people: "To the child, the genius with imagination, or the wholly untraveled the approach to a great city for the first time is a wonderful thing. Particularly if it be evening - that mystic period between the glare and the gloom of the world when life is changing from one sphere or condition to another. Ah, the promise of the night." Even the toilers, those still shut up in the shops, seem to be caught up in this evening illusion of lights popping on everywhere, people hustling somewhere - though both the sense of gaiety and of activity often prove, at least for the many toilers, to be false. "I shall soon be free." With insight, Dreiser expresses the worker's "old illusion of hope" nightly reborn.

Yet it is a frightened Carrie, in spite of reassurances at a discreet distance from Mr. Drouet, who steps into the "perfunctory embrace" of her sister with the unmistakable air of "the grimness of shift and toil." "She felt cold reality taking her by the hand. No world of light and merriment. No round of amusement."

Comment

Several important **themes** and ideas are established in Chapter One which the reader must carry with him into subsequent chapters. One is materialism, the impact and influence of money and the power which comes with money. To the have-nots of any period, the power of money and material things cannot be overestimated: this **theme** Dreiser intends to drive home throughout the novel.

Another "force" - almost a personality - is the city itself and its conditions, especially its conditions as contrasted between rich and poor. To Dreiser - and to a number of his contemporaries: Thomas Hardy in England, Frank, Norris in America - the city (or rather, rapid industrialization of our civilization accompanied by exploitation of workers through long hours and low wages) came to represent the large part environment plays in the shaping of individual destinies. In other words, Dreiser stresses such deterministic forces over free will. All of the authors of this period, who were protesting social conditions, constantly reiterated the term "determinism," the idea that when environment is a controlling factor, when power is concentrated in the hands of a few, a man has much less free will than he might imagine.

Note that it is one of Dreiser's habits of style to intermix with his dialogue and his description of characters rather purely reflective passages. For example, in Chapter One, "Lest this order of individual should permanently pass, let me put down some of the most striking characteristics ..."; or, "A woman should someday write the complete philosophy of clothes. No matter how young, it is one of the things she wholly comprehends"; or, "How true it is that words are but the vague shadows of the volumes we mean."

CHAPTER 2: WHAT POVERTY THREATENED: OF GRANITE AND BRASS

In sharp contrast to the world imagined by Carrie's new friend Drouet, is the "drag of a lean and narrow life" which she perceives on arriving at the flat of her sister, Minnie Hanson. Carrie, with "some slight gift of observation and that sense, so rich in every woman-intuition," responds to the nature of Mr. Hanson, a quiet second-generation Swede "of a clean, saving disposition." It is Hanson's manner, in fact, which sets the whole atmosphere of the flat. Carrie's sister has become a woman "with ideas of life colored by her husband's, and fast hardening into narrower conceptions of pleasure and duty than had ever been hers in a thoroughly circumscribed youth."

It is obvious that the narrowed conception of life and pleasure, which pervades the Hanson flat and dampens Carrie's timid enthusiasm, is closely related to that Chicago of 1889 which Dreiser now pauses to comment on: that "giant magnet, drawing to itself, from all quarters, the hopeful and the hopeless - those who had their fortune yet to make and those whose fortunes and affairs had reached a disastrous **climax** elsewhere." One characteristic peculiar to Chicago of the late 1800s was its sprawling industrial growth. Its rapidly developing wholesale and shopping district, for example, spread itself out amply and impressively, for there was space, literal space, available. Such a situation made possible a front-window facade of luxury, behind which the grimy sweatshops lurked. "The entire metropolitan center possessed a high and mighty air calculated to overawe and abash the common applicant, and to make the gulf between poverty and success seem both wide and deep."

Comment

Dreiser is always calculating to foreshadow the future fate of his characters who are - and will be - caught in the great magnet. Thus he emphasizes both the actual great gulf between poverty and success in Chicago in 1899, and the even greater gulf between her poor, small self and the pressing sense of power which bears down on Carrie from the granite buildings and chills her hesitating hand on the brass doorknobs. Dreiser is telling us that the realities of the case were indeed grim but that Carrie's untutored imaginings were in fact almost paralyzing: "She walked bravely forward, led by an honest desire to find employment and delayed at every step by the interest of the unfolding scene, and a sense of helplessness amid so much evidence of power and force which she did not understand."

CHAPTER 3: WE QUESTION OF FORTUNE: FOUR-FIFTY A WEEK

Carrie's state of mind and its fluctuations, as she ventures into the wholesale and manufacturing district of Chicago seeking employment, are quite recognizable to anyone who has gone looking for his first job. Walking through the doors, asking questions, confronting managers, are not nearly so easy as the mere contemplation of doing them. She soon becomes painfully aware of her insignificance and her poverty. "To avoid a certain indefinable shame she felt at being caught spying about for a position she quickened her steps and assumed an air of indifference supposedly common to one upon an errand." Carrie is acutely - and quite naturally - self-conscious. Her first encounter with a job manager, however, is pleasant enough to cause her to reflect: that "she had not been put to shame and made to feel her unfortunate position, seemed remarkable."

Subsequent contacts prove less pleasant, however, and Carrie vaguely turns her attention to the department stores, which might be hiring shopgirls. The vagueness of her search here is aptly described. "Some time she spent in wandering up and down, thinking to encounter the buildings by chance, so readily is the mind, bent upon prosecuting a hard but needful errand, eased by that self-deception which the semblance of search, without the reality, gives." But the department stores with their vast variety of economic dazzle (so familiar to the reader of today but, at that past period, a flowering phenomenon), are quite out of Carrie's reach, either for purchasing or for employment. "A flame of envy lighted in her heart. She realized in a dim way how much the city held - wealth, fashion, ease - every adornment for women, and she longed for dress and beauty with a whole heart." Even the shopgirls present a smart, sophisticated appearance with which Carrie's worn apparel compares sadly.

At length Carrie is offered a very poor position by some manufacturers of boys' caps, at $3.50 per week. Desperate and exhausted as she has begun to feel, she cannot believe that she will have to take this job. It is in her "wearisome, baffled retreat" to Minnie's flat that she notices a middle-aged gentleman at a desk inside a large wholesale shoe house; and, on "one of those forlorn impulses which often grow out of a fixed sense of defeat," Carrie walks through this last door, inquires, and thus comes away with a job paying $4.50 a week. She accepts this sum, in her fatigue of body and spirit, though she had expected $6.00.

Dreiser closes this chapter by adroitly depicting Carrie's pathetic (because so false and ill-founded) lift in spirits: "Her nervous tension relaxed. She walked out into the busy street and discovered a new atmosphere.... She noticed that men and women were smiling.... This was a great pleasing metropolis after all. Her new firm was a goodly institution. Its windows were of huge plate glass."

Comment

Dreiser has done superbly two things in Chapter 3. He has underlined the realities of the gap between success and poverty in Chicago in 1899, which may be taken as the prototype for the situation in other industrializing centers of the United States during that period. And through unfaltering, humane psychological **realism**, he has given us a picture of the fluctuating mind of Carrie Meeber, a picture which centers upon the conflicts that will dominate her thinking about this new environment and her place in it.

Dreiser has now initiated a "critical parallelism" which is worth noting. Just as he illuminated in Chapter 1 the gap between instinct and reason (**foreshadowing** the conflict between the two which was even then developing in Carrie's mind), so in this chapter he underscores the gap between success and poverty. There is another "gap" illustrated in this chapter too: the gap between Carrie's imaginings about her success in jobhunting, and the reality of the job she ultimately gets. It is important to realize three things at this point in the novel. (1) Dreiser considers both the "gaps" and his characters' responses to them as psychologically real and natural. (2) The conflicts caused by these internal and external forces will be developed and amplified throughout the book. (3) There is, of course, a close parallelism between these external forces - what the granite and brass of Chicago represent in terms of success and poverty (and in each chapter this picture of the city is enlarged, whether to include the department stores or the residential districts or the open, parklike spaces) - and the internal forces (Carrie's fantasies of material success vs. Carrie's actualities; Carrie's early - and lingering - conflict between some sense of duty and conventional morality vs. her deep-rooted desire for pleasure). We can expect the author to continue exploring these disparities in the world of Carrie, the resulting conflicts, and how they are resolved. To put it another way, Dreiser is very concerned with the difference between what a person's imagination conceives and what he is able to actually realize, or, simply stated, that difference between what a person wants, and what he gets, out of life. There are circumstances, Dreiser says, beyond the average person's control (or even the above-average person's, since we see Carrie as somewhat superior to her lovers in sensitivity) which shape his fate, even though he may be vaguely, imperfectly - and almost always, impotently - aware of such forces.

CHAPTER 4: THE SPENDINGS OF FANCY: FACTS ANSWER WITH SNEERS

The humanness and the **irony** of Carrie's situation are rather well combined in this chapter, which spans the period of the weekend days of her impossible fantasies about the material gain and pleasure she anticipates from her new position and her first workday. During these three days Carrie also gains insight into what is "approved" or "disapproved" in the sphere of the Hansons and their flat. Finding a job on the first day of searching is approved, but expressing a desire to attend H. R. Jacob's, a noted theatre of melodrama nearby, is disapproved as wanton expenditure of money which ought to be saved. We find out something significant about Carrie's character here, in her surprising insistence upon going to the theatre that night. "Naturally timid in all things that related to her own advancement, and especially so when without power or resource, her craving for pleasure was so strong that it was the one stay of her nature. She would speak for that when silent on all else." Dreiser suggests that this is both a craving for pleasure born of deprivation, and an instinctual craving (as he develops it later in Drouet and in Hurstwood).

Contrasted to Carrie's fancies and the desire for pleasure (which is not, of course, gratified on that occasion) is the initiation into that "solemn round of industry" - which the Hansons have by now accepted as inevitable in their lives - on her first day of work at a machine which punches eyeholes in the upper part of a man's shoe. It is, again, a human scene. Carrie in her nervous anxiety expends too much energy on the simple task. The girls at her right and left realize her nervousness and try to help her with delaying tactics. The hours drag out interminably as only they can when one sits hunched over on a high, backless stool performing an alien function. The lunch break emphasizes for Carrie, as she listens to the gossip of the girls and their banter back and forth with the men, her isolation from these people who are low and common. Our Carrie is indeed several cuts above these young persons in the shoe manufacturing shop. But as she observes them in their uncouth remarks and their sloppy dress, we are told (ironically) that, in such conclusions, she "made the average feminine distinction between clothes, putting worth, goodness, and distinction in a dress suit, and leaving all the unlovely qualities and those beneath notice in overalls and jumper." This we are to recall upon the subsequent entrance of Drouet and, later, Hurstwood.

Comment

Dreiser is almost outspoken here (as he will be elsewhere) in his ironic criticism of the prevailing "social theories" of the day, remarking that "under better material conditions, this kind of work would not have been so bad, but the new socialism which involves pleasant working conditions for employees had not then taken told upon manufacturing companies." The working rooms smelled unpleasantly of oil, leather and other, staler, odors. The floor was continually littered. "Not the slightest provision had been made for the comfort of the employees, the idea being that something was gained by giving them as little and making the work as hard and unremunerative as possible. What we know of footrests, swivelback chairs, dining rooms for the girls, clean aprons and curling irons supplied free, and a decent cloakroom, were unthought of. The washrooms were disagreeable, crude, if not foul places, and the whole atmosphere was sordid." The author is simply pointing out that it is little wonder, really, that Carrie on her way home at the long day's end reflects that "she should be better served, and her heart revolted."

CHAPTER 5: A GLITTERING NIGHT FLOWER: THE USE OF A NAME

It is fitting (and a sound novelistic technique) that we turn now to a consideration of Charles Drouet - what he likes, the way he spends his days, who his associates are. His hierarchy of values is further illuminated in this chapter. At the same time, there is the introduction of G. W. Hurstwood, and a rather detailed account of Chicago's restaurants and bars in 1900 ... Rector's, and Fitzgerald and Moy's, which figures more largely in the story as Hurstwood's place of employ.

G. W. Hurstwood, to the genial hustler Drouet, is "someone worth knowing"; "he had been pointed out as a very successful and well-known man about town." He is of interest to the reader, though, not only as Carrie's second lover but as a type different from Drouet, indeed as a representative of a class above Drouet in the social system that focused on material things. Hurstwood "had a good, stout constitution, an active manner, and a solid, substantial air which was composed in part of his fine clothes, his clean linen, his jewels, and, above all, his own sense of his importance... . He was shrewd and clever in many little things, and capable of creating a good impression. His managerial position was fairly important-a kind of stewardship which was imposing, but lacked financial control."

The account of Hurstwood's daily activities as manager of Fitzgerald and Moy's is interesting as a commentary on human nature in general and on his society in particular. It is important to Hurstwood, for instance, to know by name and greet personally "hundreds of actors, merchants, politicians and the general run of successful characters-about-town." He has "a finely graduated scale of informality and friendship." For his hierarchy of acquaintances and friends he summons forth a hierarchy of greetings. The significant exception to his show of good-fellowship is that class "too rich, too famous, or too successful, with whom he could not attempt any familiarity of address, and with these he was professionally tactful, assuming a grave and dignified attitude, paying them the deference which would win their good feeling without in the least compromising his own bearing and opinions." Hurstwood is, then, a shrewder and more calculating person than Drouet; and he is already more "successful."

There are those with whom Hurstwood is "friendly on the score of good-fellowship," however, and Drouet is among them. These two men like each other, although Drouet is merely a "successful" traveling salesman, whereas Hurstwood has made himself into "a very acceptable individual of our great American upper class-the first grade below the luxuriously rich." As the story progresses we see how Hurstwood's family is thus destined-inevitably-to a frustrated competition with those luxuriously rich.

Dreiser concludes this chapter with interesting observations on an "institution" such as Fitzgerald and Moy's (its modern counterpart is the "in" bar or cocktail lounge of every American city of any size), and comments on Drouet's place in such surroundings. Drouet of course is one of the "moths," Dreiser says, who come "in endless procession, to bask in the light of the flame." And we note, remembering Sister Carrie's similar craving, that he "was lured as much by his longing for pleasure as by his desire to shine among his betters."

Comment

In his description of the barroom and his analysis of what motivates its habitues. Dreiser is at pains to distinguish between what is "social" and what is "sinful." As a matter of fact, the idea of "sin" hardly enters in, since the tone he affects and the terms he chooses are really "nonmoral." He realizes, for example, that it is neither intellectual stimulation nor political bargaining nor actual thirst for liquor which drives these people to their favored bar; he concludes that it "must be that a strange bundle of passions and vague desires give rise to such a curious social institution or it would not be." But it is essential to recognize Dreiser's nonmoralizing attitude here, since it prevails for the most part throughout the novel (and since it constitutes some of the grounds on which the novel, when released in 1900, was considered objectionable). Drouet and his friends dropped in at Fitzgerald and Moy's "because they craved, without, perhaps, consciously analyzing it, the company, the glow, the atmosphere which they found. One might take it, after all, as an augur of the better social order, for the things which they satisfied here, though sensory, were not evil. No evil could come out of the contemplation of an expensively decorated chamber. The worst effect of such a thing would be, perhaps, to stir up in the material-minded an ambition to arrange their lives upon a similarly splendid basis. In the last analysis, that would scarcely be called the fault of the decorations, but rather of the innate trend of the mind." In effect Dreiser is saying what a well-known medieval maxim expressed long ago: "Honi soit qui mal y pense." (He who thinks it is evil makes it so.)

CHAPTER 6: THE MACHINE AND THE MAIDEN: A KNIGHT OF TODAY

"At the flat that evening Carrie felt a new phase of its atmosphere. The fact that it was unchanged, while her feelings were different, increased her knowledge of its character." Thus, in her response to her environs, Carrie proves herself a regular little pragmatist. [A pragmatist, briefly defined, is a person who is able to put aside his ideas of what "should" be or what he "wishes" were true in the face of what is: he can assess the things that happen in life more practically, seeing them as they actually are as contrasted to what he might have expected them to be.] There is no jolly welcome or warmth of approval awaiting Carrie in Hanson's stolid flat: "These were the things upon which her mind ran, and it was like meeting with opposition at every turn to find no one here to call forth or respond to her feelings." Such feelings of opposition, of course, set the stage for Carrie's receptiveness to Drouet when he reappears.

Yet, informed as readers that "when she was trimly dressed she was rather a sweet little being, with large eyes and a sad mouth. Her face expressed the mingled expectancy, dissatisfaction, and depression she felt," we cannot help but feel sympathy toward her; and we avoid judgment when told that "her imagination trod a very narrow round, always, winding up at points which concerned money, looks, clothes, or enjoyment." Such responses we more and more see are "determined" by all past and present circumstances. For Carrie is "better" than her surroundings. The reader sympathizes with her subsequent days of drudgery at the factory, her earnings completely eaten up by necessities, culminating in the sickness brought on by insufficient clothing in the wintering weather and in the loss of her position.

In such a state of spreading discontent she re-encounters Charles Drouet, who offers food, money and good fellowship, all with a kind of innocence he himself partially believes in. She dines with him at an established and well-appointed restaurant. That the "little soldier of fortune took her good turn in an easy way" comes as no surprise, since ignorant and innocent Carrie is inclined, especially when in desperate need, to take such favors as they come. Drouet is a brotherly type, in that he instinctively sympathizes with women besides pursuing them: and in this instance his "liberality and good humor" affect them both favorably. Drouet's offer of money, consequently, when he perceives her grim situation, is at this point a virtually innocent extension of his goodwill toward a pretty and plaintive girl. "I'll help you," he asserts; and she leaves him "feeling as though a great arm had slipped out before her to draw off trouble. The money she had accepted was two soft, green, handsome ten-dollar bills." But again, although in a nonmoralizing way, Dreiser makes us see that our heroine's future rides on these soft, green, handsome bills: it is the soft voice of the serpent of the city and of inner human nature speaking.

Comment

As Carrie stands downstairs at the door in frustration and boredom, her brother-in-law comes downstairs. "While Hanson really came for bread, the thought dwelt with him that now he would see what Carrie was doing. No sooner did he draw near her with that in mind than she felt it. Of course, she had no understanding of what put it into her head, but, nevertheless, it aroused in her the first shade of real antipathy to him. She knew now that she did not like him. He was suspicious... . A thought will color a world for us." The point to be made here is that Dreiser takes trouble to record rather accurately the flux of Carrie's mind. In so doing he may be called a precursor, if not a practitioner, of modern "stream of consciousness." That is, he describes in some detail Carrie's sequences of thought, her changing consciousness of her world. This author is, in any case, an astute observer and recorder of the imagination and emotions of his characters.

CHAPTER 7: THE LURE OF THE MATERIAL: BEAUTY SPEAKS FOR ITSELF

The curious, philosophizing passage which introduces this chapter seems to say: Money is not the root of all evil, after all, although one's conscious or unconscious attitudes toward it may propel one to disaster. Again, Honi soit qui mal y pense. We shall return to this passage later. Dreiser's efforts here are to establish that Carrie and Drouet, although they may be weak, indecisive, and unreflecting, are not evil. Carrie's response to the money she has accepted from Drouet is at this point direct, untroubled by moral implications. "She felt that she was immensely better off for the having of them. It was something that was power in itself." This sense of power Carrie feels is central to our future understanding of her actions, for her conditioning toward money has been the common one: "Money: something everybody else has and that I must get." Similarly, it is essential to recognize that Drouet is actually a good-hearted fellow. For example, Dreiser poses the interesting hypothetical situation of Drouet's being approached by a beggar: "He would gladly have handed out what was considered the proper portion to give beggars and thought no more about it. There would have been no speculation, no philosophizing." We will recall this comment later on the occasion of Carrie's theatrical performance, when the three-Carrie, Hurstwood, and Drouet-are leaving the theatre and are confronted by a beggar. The author points out: "A truly deep-dyed villain could have hornswoggled him as readily as he could have flattered a pretty shopgirl. His fine success as a salesman lay in his geniality and the thoroughly reputable standing of his house. He bobbed about among men, a veritable bundle of enthusiasm-no power worthy the name of intellect, no thoughts worthy the adjective noble, no feelings long continued in one strain." But perhaps the reader is being urged at this point to ask this question: If there is that quality of calculation and reflection in Hurstwood, can we also suspect that there is some quality of evil?

Carrie makes a pretense to herself of going shopping with the money she has in her pocket, enjoying that "middle state in which we mentally balance at times, possessed of the means, lured by desire, and yet deterred by conscience or want of decision." Although the statement applies directly to her expenditures on new clothes, we can see that this state of indecision may figure largely in Carrie's larger destiny too. For in this instance she meets Drouet, whose cheerful presence easily banishes her doubts. Drouet again responds to that as yet indefinable difference between Carrie and other young women he has known: "She was a sweet little mortal to him-there was no doubt of that. She seemed to have some power back of her actions. She was not like the common run of store girls. She wasn't silly." Dreiser reinforces this difference (because it will help us understand Carrie's later actions): "In reality, Carrie had more imagination than he-more taste. It was a finer mental strain in her that made possible her depression and loneliness. Her poor clothes were neat, and she held her head unconsciously in a dainty way." Carrie is a young woman of potential, then; and we wonder how it will develop as the chapter concludes with her hesitant decision to pack up and leave Minnie's flat, secretly, for the room Drouet has found for her.

Comment

In the opening sentences of this chapter Dreiser seems to be commenting in general on what he considers the "money morality" of his American society in 1900. He intimates that he himself may still be looking, reflectively, for the answer as to why there is both a "money morality" and a "money guilt." "The true meaning of money yet remains to be popularly explained and comprehended. When each individual realizes for himself that this thing primarily stands for and should only be accepted as a moral due-that it should be paid out as honestly stored energy, and not as a usurped privilege-many of our social, religious, and political troubles will have permanently passed." The significant terms here are "moral due," "honestly stored energy," and "usurped privilege." He is introducing the idea that there are, in fact, money rights. For example a man's work should not be his punishment (which is the light in which we are led to view the sweatshops), but should be his decent earning of what is rightfully his due. This being the case, money earned carries with it a right to be spent-or at least used-with a feeling of satisfaction rather than of the guilt of "a usurped privilege."

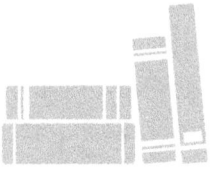

SISTER CARRIE

TEXTUAL ANALYSIS

CHAPTERS 8-18

CHAPTER 8: INTIMATIONS BY WINTER: AN AMBASSADOR SUMMONED

The reflections which open this chapter are often referred to as basic to Dreiser's philosophy of "determinism" - deterministic forces which shape the lives of men. He asserts that "among the forces which sweep and play throughout the universe, untutored man is but a wisp in the wind. Our civilization is still in a middle stage, scarcely beast, in that it is no longer wholly guided by instinct; scarcely human, in that it is not yet wholly guided by reason." This is the conflict he has already introduced, between instinct and reason; now he expands it. But its basic tenet is that man is "even as a wisp in the wind, moved by every breath of passion, acting now by his will and now by his instincts, erring with one, only to retrieve by the other, falling by one, only to rise by the other-a creature of incalculable variability." (The modern reader, incidentally, may find it a bit hard to agree with Dreiser's conclusion here: "We have the consolation of knowing that evolution is ever in action, that the ideal is a light that cannot fail... . The needle of understanding will yet point steadfast and unwavering to the distant pole of truth." His prophecy is somewhat wishful, since in our time the needle of understanding is still none too steadfast.)

Carrie again reacts "pragmatically" to her new situation, in that she sees possibilities in it. "She turned about, troubled by her daring, glad of her release, wondering whether she would get something to do, wondering what Drouet would do." Neither she nor Drouet realizes how far the circumstances are already set, how much they are already caught, unconsciously, in their own wandering, unreflecting webs. For we are told that Drouet, too, now "had his future fixed for him beyond a peradventure. He could not help what he was going to do. He could not see clearly enough to wish to do differently. He was drawn by his innate desire to act the old pursuing part. He would need to delight himself with Carrie as surely as he would need to eat his heavy breakfast." Dreiser is politely saying that however much each of them may vaguely imagine that they are going to sustain a Platonic relationship, it is now a certainty that Carrie will become Drouet's mistress and live with him.

There is another significant passage in this chapter, colored humanely with pathos by the author. If the novel were a drama, the reader might pause here and say, "Ah, if the tragic heroine had stopped here, she might have been saved." It involves the question of habits, some kind of discipline so established by the past that it might guide even the unreflective person to safer ground. The hour is late when Drouet and Carrie finish their after-theatre lunch, and "just a shade of a thought of the hour entered Carrie's head, but there was no household law to govern her now. If any habits ever had time to fix upon her, they would have operated here. Habits are peculiar things. They will drive the really nonreligious mind out of bed to say prayers that are only a custom and not a devotion. The victim of habit, when he has neglected the thing which it was his custom to do, feels a little scratching in the brain, a little irritating something which comes of being out of the rut, and imagines it to be the prick of conscience, the still, small voice that is urging him ever to righteousness." (Dreiser's **irony**, of course, is also clear when he adds that the "drag of habit" may be enough to cause the "unreasoning victim to return and perform the perfunctory thing." He makes it clear that in so doing, the "victim" has not really done his duty as he imagines, but has merely done again a habitual thing!)

Aside from the **irony** here, the author is also saying that, forgetting about free will for the moment, if a girl like Carrie had been sufficiently dragged back by some small disciplines of past habit, her destiny might have been different. But "Carrie had no excellent home principles fixed upon her. If she had, she would have been more consciously distressed." There is an implication here that poverty operates in a vicious circle which encourages the conflicts we see in the characters of this novel. People from impoverished backgrounds enjoy neither the satisfactions of "excellent home principles" nor of material well-being.

Another indication that the author wishes this chapter to stand as a crucial one-a turning point-is Minnie's troubled dream about Sister Carrie, wherein there appears to be a simple symbolism. Minnie imagines in her sleep that Carrie is sinking into a deep black pit of a coal mine, and later, that her fingers are slipping in their hold on a rock as she falls into deep water. It is an understated instance of "intuition" on the part of Minnie.

Comment

The opening passage of this chapter, however deterministic it is in essence, also suggests an underlying current of idealism in Dreiser's thought: man cannot "forever balance thus between good and evil," and the "ideal is a light that cannot fail." We can suggest several explanations for such idealism on Dreiser's part: (1) It may be a simple expression of his personal idealism, his faith in the innate goodness of man. (2) Such a faith in man's innate goodness, however, also recalls the period (socio-economic, political and literary) which just preceded Dreiser's time: the Romantic Movement. Though it came to a close about 1830 in England and Europe, this period lasted several decades longer in America, with its ideal view of man and of his capacities for good. (3) It may be, then, that, influenced as he is by the harsher deterministic thinking of his own time, Dreiser also nostalgically recalls a past period of idealism; thus he may be rationalizing or sentimentalizing a bit here. Dreiser's critics have been known to criticize him for his sentimentality.

CHAPTER 9: CONVENTION'S OWN TINDERBOX: THE EYE THAT IS GREEN

This chapter, devoted to G. W. Hurstwood's home life, constructs an image of him, too, as just another character (although in a different class) who will, probably, become a confused and passive participant in predetermined effects. Dreiser in his descriptions begins deceptively: "A lovely home atmosphere is one of the flowers of the world, than which there is nothing more tender, nothing more delicate, nothing more calculated to make strong and just the natures cradled and nourished within it." Then, while the reader is mulling over the pleasing philosophic truth of this passage, the author shatters the ideal image above with the stark, ironic statement that "Hurstwood's residence could scarcely be said to be infused with this home spirit. It lacked that toleration and regard without which the home is nothing."

In the pages following the reader is made to see unmistakably the sterility of Hurstwood's life, from his "perfectly appointed house," to his completely self-involved son and daughter, to his wife who is a stereotyped and selfish social climber. "The atmosphere which such personalities would create must be apparent to all. It worked out in a thousand little conversations, all of which were of the same caliber" - that is to say, shallow, as Dreiser so incisively demonstrates in the dinner table exchanges here recorded. In the midst of this atmosphere we learn, not surprisingly, that Hurstwood had "a tendency in him to walk away from the impossible thing." His was not a nature "to trouble for something better, unless the better was immediately and sharply contrasted. As it was, he received and gave, irritated sometimes by the little displays of selfish indifference, pleased at times by some show of finery which supposedly made for dignity and social distinction. The life of the resort which he managed was his life." And as to his relations with his wife, we are told bluntly. "There was no love lost between them. There was no great feeling of dissatisfaction." Hurstwood's philosophy at this point seems to be the preservation of a clean respectability, which makes him "circumspect" in all that he does: "A man can't be too careful."

But Dreiser concludes the chapter by marking the thought he previewed in the title, "convention's own tinderbox." He enlarges the figurative image: "Such an atmosphere could hardly come under the category of home life. It ran along by force of habit, by force of conventional opinion. With the lapse of time, it must necessarily become dryer and dryer-must eventually be tinder, easily lighted and destroyed.

Comment

It is clear from this chapter that Dreiser intends to consider- and criticize-many aspects of American society of the 1890s. Here he has emphasized a thought he will expand: The sterile **conventions** sustained by a materialistic, unreflective society do not build qualities of character capable of much "toleration and regard," without which, indeed, man is as a "wisp in the wind" of forces external to himself.

CHAPTER 10: THE COUNSEL OF WINTER: FORTUNE'S AMBASSADOR CALLS

Since the author has just made it clear in the foregoing chapter that his is an adversely critical attitude toward "convention," when it is sustained by selfish or unreflective people out of habits of social conformity, it is none too surprising that he opens here with carefully ironic reflections on Carrie: "In the light of the world's attitude toward woman and her duties, the nature of Carrie's mental state deserves consideration. Actions such as hers are measured by an arbitrary scale. Society possesses a conventional standard whereby it judges all things. All men should be good, all women virtuous. Wherefore, villain, has thou failed?" (The "villain," of course is "society" - but let us not press this identification too far at the moment, else we may lose sight of the many, many aspects of that society which

Dreiser is going to present to us.) He concludes, "We have but an infantile perception of morals," and his own position is, as usual, nonmoralizing.

Nevertheless, we are not permitted to forget that there is still conflict in Carrie's mind about her present situation: her mental world is currently less pretty to her than her exterior surroundings. She has a conscience, but it exhibits no philosopher's powers. Dreiser is asking, indeed, why Carrie's conscience should be better than average, when he ironically comments, "It was no just and sapient counselor, in its last analysis. It was only an average little conscience, a thing which represented the world, her past environment, habit, **convention**, in a confused way. With it, the voice of the people was truly the voice of God." It is, of course, quite psychologically insightful and ruthlessly realistic of the author to depict Carrie's "conscience" not as some innate, God-given, abstract power but as a product of her external environment. And we note that, given mental conflict, "Carrie had not the mind to get firm hold upon a definite truth. When she could not find her way out of the labyrinth of illogic which thought upon the subject created, she would turn away entirely." Thus we are aware that neither Carrie nor Drouet nor Hurstwood is a character capable of concentrating for long on hard thoughts or impossible conflicts.

Other ideas dropped throughout the chapter pave the way for the entrance of Hurstwood. Carrie is not really in love with Drouet; she is in fact "more clever than he," and has begun to perceive dimly his deficiencies. Drouet himself is limited by his very egotism in reaching the accomplishments and self-possession of a Hurstwood, and he is liable to fail "dismally where the woman was slightly experienced and possessed innate refinement." (These passages, incidentally, serve to verify Dreiser's realistic insights into the psychology of men and women.) Thus the evening which Hurstwood spends with Carrie and Drouet heavily foreshadows the future, beginning with Carrie's inevitable comparison of the two men who sit before her.

Comment

Note that from Hurstwood's suggestion, "Suppose we have a little game of euchre?" there is a clever parallelism between the card game and the developing competitive situation, sustained by the dialogue. Carrie "doesn't know how to play," and Hurstwood calculates not only to teach her, good-humoredly, but to let her win. It is clear that Hurstwood has entered the "game," and that he intends if he can (and he is capable of it) to outwit Drouet - and, indeed, Carrie herself.

CHAPTER 11: THE PERSUASION OF FASHION: FEELING GUARDS O'ER ITS OWN

"Carrie was an apt student of fortune's ways-of fortune's superficialities. Seeing a thing, she would immediately set to inquiring how she would look, properly related to it. Be it known that this is not fine feeling, it is not wisdom. The greatest minds are not so afflicted; and, on the contrary, the lowest order of mind is not so disturbed. Fine clothes to her were a vast persuasion; they spoke tenderly and Jesuitically for themselves. When she came within earshot of their pleading, desire in her bent a willing ear." This brilliant opening is designed to set the stage for the success of Hurstwood with Carrie. Even Drouet, in his bright approval of her developing taste-as indeed he admires readily all that is pretty in all women - "weakens her power" of resisting the persuasions of fashion and her own reflection which she finds more and more pleasing in the mirror.

In this chapter we see the beginning of feelings in Carrie which are familiarly female but disastrous to a relationship. On a particular afternoon, lulled into melancholy by sentimental music drifting through her open door, Carrie, ever the wisp in the atmospheric wind, has "reverted to the things which were best and saddest within the small limit of her experience. She became for the moment a repentant." But Drouet rushes through his doorway in the late afternoon in an entirely different mood and, noticing tears in her eyes, sets about good-naturedly (for he erroneously attributes her depression, egotistically, to her loneliness for him) to dispel the gloom: "Come on, now, it's all right. Let's waltz a little to that music." As Dreiser puts it with dry humor, "He could not have introduced a more incongruous proposition. It made clear to Carrie that he could not sympathize with her…. It was his first great mistake." Thus Carrie is ready to go to better things. Upon Hurstwood's determined reappearance, Drouet perceives nothing amiss: "He had no power of analyzing the glance and the atmosphere of a man like Hurstwood."

Dreiser resumes the **metaphor** of the "game," adding to it the heat of "battle." Again, as they emerge from the theatre and bid Hurstwood goodnight, with Carrie observing that she has had "such a nice time," the author manages both **irony** and wit: "'Yes, indeed,' added Drouet, who was not in the least aware that a battle had been fought and his defenses weakened. He was like the Emperor of China who sat glorying in himself, unaware that his fairest provinces were being wrested from him." On their way home in the trolley car, unconscious of Carrie's mental activities comparing the two men she has spent the evening with, "he foolishly went to the forward platform of the car and left the game as it stood."

Comment

We must note here how natural the author makes Carrie's gradual desertion to the other camp seem. This is due to Hurstwood's shrewdness and coolness of experience. (His life, both public and private, as we now know, has little of the foundation of "toleration and regard.") Other factors are Drouet's prevailing egotism (which of course obscures his awareness of complicated feelings in others), his lack of calculation or analytical power, Carrie's "innate refinement," and her lack of actual experience in the sophisticated world.

CHAPTER 12: OF THE LAMP OF THE MANSIONS: THE AMBASSADOR'S PLEA

This chapter treats of the nature of Mrs. Hurstwood. Dreiser's sense of **irony** triumphs over any sense of the sentimental, in labeling her once and for all as "a cold, self-centered woman, with many a thought of her own which never found expression,..." The chapter also suggests the growing alienation between Mr. and Mrs. Hurstwood. Upon discovering that her husband has been to the theatre recently in the company of others than herself, she immediately arranges her own "trip" downtown, whereby Hurstwood is coerced into joining the party. Mrs. Hurstwood is cool and detached toward her husband, but "not at all inclined to accept anything less than a complete fulfillment of the letter of their relationship, though the spirit might be wanting."

Meanwhile, as Hurstwood's interest in Carrie increases, her fascination with him and her glimpse of the world he seems to represent grow correspondingly. Confronted with this expanding horizon, Carrie "did not grow in knowledge so much as she awakened in the matter of desire." Her association with another tenant of the house, Mrs. Hale, kindles further material desires. When Carrie returns from a drive with Mrs. Hale along North Shore Drive, whose mansions she admired, she is in a pensive mood and mindful once more of her own insignificance in that great world. Thus she is a sitting duck for Hurstwood's arrival on the scene; for he at this point "has had the advantage of practice and knows he has sympathy." When Hurstwood terminates his afternoon call on Carrie, he feels assured of his impact on her. And Carrie herself can only reflect, "I'm getting terrible," being honestly affected by a feeling of trouble and shame. "I don't seem to do anything right."

Comment

This may be treated as a transitional chapter which attempts to trace the patterns of the disintegration of relationships (Carrie's and Drouet's; Mr. and Mrs. Hurstwood's) with the corresponding natural pull of the discontented parties toward more sympathetic poles.

CHAPTER 13: HIS CREDENTIAL'S ACCEPTED: A BABEL OF TONGUES

Dreiser here attempts to record Hurstwood's reaction to Carrie honestly and realistically. He makes it clear that the fate of Drouet (losing Carrie) was one that actually rested on his own personality. Of Hurstwood, he points out that "a man in his situation who comes, after a long round of worthless or hardening experiences, upon a young, unsophisticated, innocent soul is apt either to hold aloof out of a sense of his own remoteness, or to draw near and become fascinated and elated by his discovery." The truth is that Carrie has turned out to be quite a different thing from the "baggage" with whom Hurstwood went to Drouet's house originally to spend a light evening; for she had "nothing of the art of the courtesan. He saw at once that a mistake had been made, that some difficult conditions had pushed this troubled creature into his presence, and his interest was enlisted. Here sympathy sprang to the rescue, but it was not unmixed with selfishness. He wanted to win Carrie because he thought her fate mingled with his was better than if it were united with Drouet's. He envied the drummer his conquest as he had never envied any man in all the course of his experience."

Carrie, in the meantime, has cause to reflect on what she owes to Drouet. She credits him with assisting her immensely; she looks upon him with kindness and assesses his geniality; but she "cannot feel any binding influence keeping her for him as against all others." Carrie's evaluation of Drouet is perceptive: he "carried the doom of all enduring relationships in his own lightsome manner and unstable fancy. He went merrily on, assured that he was alluring all, that affection followed tenderly in his wake, that things would endure unchangingly for his pleasure." As has been intimated previously, Drouet's essential egotism excludes him from relating closely to other human beings. And in the pages following, Hurstwood pays a determined court to Carrie, emerging with a pledge of love in response to his own.

Comment

This is one of the chapters in which the active pace predominates. Instead of lengthy descriptive or reflective passages, there is rapid dialogue. Dreiser's technical skill is seen in his being able to propel the action in strictly dramatic fashion when desirable for the development of the novel. Much of Chapter 13, for instance, could be directly translated into drama.

CHAPTER 14: WITH EYES AND NOT SEEING: ONE INFLUENCE WANES

As an added aspect of the changing picture, Carrie sees her prospective defection to Hurstwood as a way out of dishonor: she believes he will marry her. It is ironic that simultaneous with these imaginings of Carrie are the anticipations on Hurstwood's part purely of "pleasure without responsibility. He did not feel that he was doing anything to complicate his life. His position was secure, his home life, if not satisfactory, was at least undisturbed, his personal liberty rather untrammeled. Carrie's love represented only so much added pleasure. He would enjoy this new gift over and above his ordinary allowance of pleasure."

There is another theatre party made up of Hurstwood, Drouet and Carrie. This time the interval has been filled with several meetings between Hurstwood and Carrie, letters exchanged between them, and their pledges of love. The down-and-out man who confronts them as they leave the theatre may be said to foreshadow the future as well as to elicit the separate responses he does: "The plea was that of a gaunt-faced man of about thirty, who looked the picture of privation and wretchedness. Drouet was the first to see. He handed over a dime with an upwelling feeling of pity in his heart. Hurstwood scarcely noticed the incident. Carrie quickly forgot."

> **Comment**

An "ironical situation" is produced by the play that evening. "The wife listened to the seductive voice of a lover in the absence of her husband." Drouet is induced to remark: "Served him right ... a man ought to be more attentive than that to his wife if he wants to keep her." It is perhaps a bit strained and unnecessary for Dreiser to have made his point about his characters; in any case, it is the most conventional of literary devices that the author uses here.

CHAPTER 15: THE IRK OF THE OLD TIES: THE MAGIC OF YOUTH

It is novelistic logic to turn to Hurstwood's growing estrangement from his family at this point. It coincides "with the growth of his affection for Carrie. His actions, in all that related to his family, were of the most perfunctory kind. He sat at breakfast with his wife and children, absorbed in his own fancies, which reached far without the realm of their interests." It is natural that in his state any increased demands from his wife and family - and they are increasing tangibly with her demand for a season ticket to the races - bring irritation to Hurstwood. He looks up finally, as it were, from his fantasies to find that the members of his family are going their own independent ways quite well without him. His wife and children conduct their lives much as they wish, without his knowledge of their activities. He looks on and pays the bills.

Here Dreiser pauses to paint a picture of Carrie as we find her now: certainly with former defects of dress and manner rubbed away, but with undertones of innocence and many lingering illusions. "Even now she lacked self-assurance, but there was that in what she had already experienced which left her a little less than timid. She wanted pleasure, she wanted position, and yet she was confused as to what these things might be. Every hour the kaleidoscope of human affairs threw a new luster upon something, and therewith it became for her the desired-the all."

We are also told that, on "her spiritual side, she was rich in feeling," that in fact Hurstwood is not aware that he is "dealing with one whose feelings were as tender and as delicate as this."

Comment

In the midst of his "determinism" Dreiser seems to place emphasis on what is "natural" or "instinctive" in Carrie. By commenting that she is "rich in feeling," he seems to indicate that this is innate with her, that it is a good, possibly innocent quality, and that it is what places her above both the men she is involved with.

CHAPTER 16: A WITLESS ALADDIN: THE GATE TO THE WORLD

Drouet having decided for reasons of good business to devote more time to his lodge, Carrie finds herself quite by accident acting in a theatrical benefit staged by the local club. The chapter is chiefly devoted to the discovery in Carrie of "innate taste for imitation and no small ability. Even without practice, she could sometimes restore dramatic situations she had witnessed by recreating, before her mirror, the expressions of the various faces taking part in the scene." (It seems to be Dreiser's view, in fact, as he reflects a moment that in such stirrings and secret expressions as Carrie's, "such outworking of desire to reproduce life," lies the basis of all dramatic art.) Thus Carrie discovers herself a bit more, innocently encouraged, as she acts out a scene from the play, by Drouet's praiseful observation.

Comment

This too is a transitional and **foreshadowing** chapter, illuminating a new aspect of Carrie which we can rightly expect to be enlarged upon subsequently.

CHAPTER 17: A GLIMPSE THROUGH THE GATEWAY: HOPE LIGHTENS THE EYE

It is clear that the theatrical experience brings out in Carrie a show of spirit and enthusiasm hitherto undiscovered in her. Both of her lovers are charmed, Hurstwood mentally noting that she has "capabilities" he had not imagined. Dreiser explains this natural human response: "There is nothing so inspiring in life as the sight of a legitimate ambition, no matter how incipient. It gives color, force, and beauty to the possessor." Hurstwood sets about to oversee (unknown to the principals involved) that the affair be a smashing success, with full house, flowers sent up to the stage, etc. Carrie plunges into rehearsals, and immediately impresses those in charge as the lone member of their amateur company who possesses and can utilize any dramatic talent.

CHAPTER 18: JUST OVER THE BORDER A HAIL AND FAREWELL

This chapter depicts the scene before the play which, thanks to Hurstwood's efforts, shows forth a "well-dressed, good-natured, flatteringly-inclined audience." On Hurstwood's word it has become a full-dress affair, with four boxes taken by local dignitaries of the material world. Represented here (in Dreiser's reproduction of one more aspect of the nineteenth century American city scene) is "the circle of small fortunes and secret-order distinctions. These gentlemen Elks knew the standing of one another. They had regard for the ability which could amass a small fortune, own a nice home, keep a barouche or carriage, perhaps, wear fine clothes, and maintain a good mercantile position." Hurstwood is here in his element, since to these people he stands out as "someone whose reserve covered a mine of influence and solid financial prosperity, ... who had shrewdness and much assumption of dignity, who held an imposing and authoritative position, and commanded friendship by intuitive tact in handling people." The emphasis, as we see, uppermost in the minds of all those present at such a gathering, is on the material appearance one presents-however shaky it might be in reality.

Comment

Except for the portions which treat of Carrie and her preparations for the performance (and her fantasies about succeeding and becoming a real actress), this is Hurstwood's chapter. We see him, ironically in his element before his tragic fall." "Look at him any time within the half-hour before the curtain was up, he was a member of an eminent group-a rounded company of five or more whose stout figures, large white bosoms, and shining pins bespoke the character of their success. The gentlemen who brought their wives called out to shake hands. Seats clicked, ushers bowed while he looked blandly on. He was evidently a light among them, reflecting in his personality the ambitions of those who greeted him. He was acknowledged, fawned upon, in a way lionized. Through it all one could see the standing of the man. It was greatness in a way, small as it was." There is no **irony** in this description of Hurstwood; there is just the honest delineation of a circle, a level in society of which Hurstwood was truly a superior representative. And, particularly in the closing sentence, there is pathos. It hardly needs to be added, as a point in favor of Dreiser's modernity of psychological analysis and insight into human behavior, that one can without difficulty find modern counterparts to the above scene.

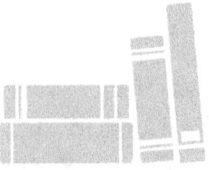

SISTER CARRIE

TEXTUAL ANALYSIS

CHAPTERS 19-32

CHAPTER 19: AN HOUR IN ELF LAND: A CLAMOR HAIF HEARD

The actual production turns out to be, naturally enough, a mixed affair, with all the actors, including Carrie, petrified into almost total ineffectuality in the first scenes. Carrie rallies, however, especially when Drouet steps backstage to encourage her, and ends by playing some of her scenes with high spirit and dramatic effect. Much space is devoted to Carrie's long, pathetic speech about love-that the one thing a woman can give or refuse is her heart. "Her beauty, her wit, her accomplishments, she may sell to you; but her love is the treasure without money and without price." If we recall the author's previous remarks that Carrie was "created with that passivity of soul which is a mirror of the actual world," that hers is the fancy to be caught by each passing moment, then we perceive the almost double **irony** here: (1) Carrie is acting well, even brilliantly; but she speaks lines about love without a concept of love upon which she could in reality act; for, as we know, she has persuaded herself she is in love with Hurstwood only because of his appearance and his compelling attentions toward her. (2) Her two lovers likewise are driven into agonies of frustrated affection by this speech; each of them, almost ludicrously, feels her lines as a direct personal appeal, yet as an appeal which neither of them will be able to answer effectively in the hard light of reality.

When the curtain goes down and Carrie's very real success is applauded, it may be said that she experiences her first true taste of independence, of power. "With the tables turned, she was looking down, rather than up."

CHAPTER 20: THE LURE OF THE SPIRIT: THE FLESH IN PURSUIT

Hurstwood, having had the past night's frustration of seeing his love home in the clutches of Drouet, is no mood for the breakfast table conflict which erupts when his wife broaches the subject of their regular summer outing. She is bent in fact upon an early departure (connected with the social aspirations of her daughter) and she impulsively concludes their argument by asserting that the family will then go without Hurstwood. It is an outburst neither of them had really anticipated, but one which had yet been brewing. It will not be forgotten by Mrs. Hurstwood.

Carrie meanwhile "had experienced a world of fancy and feeling since she had left him, the night before…. She was now experiencing the first shades of feeling of that subtle change which removes one out of the ranks of the suppliants into the lines of the dispensers of charity." Drouet likewise feels the shadow of something different upon their relationship: "Carrie was still with him, but not helpless and pleading. There was a lilt in her voice which was new." And as luck would have it, on this morning, returning to his apartment for forgotten papers and finding Carrie gone, he uncovers, through the maid, her multiple absences during his business travels, and the numerous visits of Hurstwood.

The situation is becoming emotionally loaded, the plot is moving toward points of no return for each of the three characters, and, dramatically speaking, a crisis is imminent.

CHAPTER 21: THE LURE OF THE SPIRIT: THE FLESH IN PURSUIT

Here we have Hurstwood's passion and Carrie's quandary. Hurstwood is determined to press his suit, and Carrie is in hopeless confusion: "Here was a man whom she thoroughly liked, who exercised an influence over her, sufficient almost to delude her into the belief that she was possessed of a lively passion for him. She was still the victim of his keen eyes, his suave manners, his fine clothes... . She could not resist the glow of his temperament, the light of his eye." And yet, although she does not at present realize the extent of the impossibility, of Hurstwood's silent deception, when he says, "I will arrange for you whatever," she is "struck as by a blade with the miserable provision which was outside the pale of marriage." But Hurstwood ultimately casts aside "all honesty of statement, all abandonment of truth," to promise in answer to her question that he will indeed marry her when she comes away to him on Saturday. Carrie has been swept away by the spirit of the living moment, much as she was on the stage the night before: "There had been so much enthusiasm engendered that she was believing herself deeply in love. She sighed as she thought of her handsome adorer. Yes, she would get ready by Saturday. She would go, and they would be happy."

Comment

Dreiser maintains, in this chapter and the ensuing ones, the credibility of the reader, by resorting more and more to rapidly paced dialogue intermingled but sparingly with descriptive passages or philosophic reflection. He is utilizing what is an essentially dramatic technique, limiting his prose to what is strictly functional to the quickening plot.

CHAPTER 22: THE BLAZE OF THE TINDER: FLESH WARS WITH THE FLESH

As the author dryly observes, "The misfortune of the Hurstwood household was due to the fact that jealousy, having been born of love, did not perish with it." That Hurstwood is no longer attentive to her even in their conventional social sense is enough to turn Mrs. Hurstwood's jealousy to hate; she becomes "resentful and suspicious. The jealousy that prompted her to observe every falling away from the little amenities of the married relation on his part served to give her notice of the airy grace with which he still took the world." Hurstwood virtually damns himself, for example, with his scrupulous attentions to his own personal appearance, in pursuit as he is of new pleasures.

Furthermore, in the Hurstwood family there are more and more of those little arguments, "the result of a growth of natures which were largely independent and selfish." Hurstwood, as a "man of authority and some fine feeling," is irritated "to find himself surrounded more and more by a world upon which he had no hold, and of which he had a lessening understanding." It is under these circumstances that Mrs. Hurstwood, "straining to revolt," undertakes to obtain "knowledge of something which would give her both authority and excuse." Although the only evidence she obtains is not in itself so damaging-it is the account of Hurstwood's participation in the Elks theatrical, without her-she bluffs her way through the accusation, playing her trump card for all it is worth. She demands that the money for the family outing be handed to her on the following morning; then, pressing her advantage (for Hurstwood, in the typical position of the person guilty of some sin, has no way of knowing how much she actually knows, and mistakes her bravado for information against him), she asserts that she will seek a lawyer.

CHAPTER 23: A SPIRIT IN TRAVAIL: ONE RUN PUT BEHIND

Carrie is no more in control of her situation than is Hurstwood: for as soon as she returns home from her meeting with him, her misgivings, born of lack of decision, return. She recalls that she is, after all, well situated, an "urgent matter" to one "more or less afraid of the world." Nor has Hurstwood really "taken a firm hold on her understanding"; she is in fact drawn to him mostly in his pressing presence in person or in letters. Dreiser here indulges in one of his specific yet general analyses of people, while at the same time **foreshadowing** Carrie's fate: "She might have been said to be imagining herself in love, when she was not. Women frequently do this. It flows from the fact that in each exists a bias toward affection, a craving for the pleasure of being loved. The longing to be shielded, bettered, sympathized with, is one of the attributes of the sex. This, coupled with sentiment and a natural tendency to emotion, often makes refusing difficult. It persuades them that they are in love." Just as Hurstwood has had his confrontation in the previous chapter, so Carrie is to have hers from Drouet here; nor is she in any better position to judge how much he knows. It is interesting however, that the emotional peak of her reaction comes from the revelation that Hurstwood is a married man. From that point onward her responses are unthinking, irrational, and of course damaging to the relationship between herself and Drouet. She is about to rush impulsively from the flat, when Drouet's innate good nature and general affection assert themselves, and he tries to reason with her. But "her mind was shaken loose from the little mooring of logic that it had. She was stirred by this thought, angered by that-her own injustice, Hurstwood's, Drouet's, their respective qualities of kindness and favor, the threat of the world outside in which she had failed once before, the impossibility of this state inside, where the chambers were no longer justly hers, the effect of the argument upon her nerves, ..." Drouet's compromise with her is to suggest that she stay out the month while he himself will leave immediately (all the while expecting that she will not ultimately leave). Carrie feels his interest, his gentleness, and her own regret. But we note that her answer to all his questions about what she wants or what she should do is the same, her conflicts being resolved by: "I don't know." Carrie, for all her virtues, is, by her preconditioning, truly a wisp in the wind.

CHAPTER 24: ASHES OF TINDER: A FACE AT THE WINDOW

It is meanwhile clear from the incisive actions taken by Mrs. Hurstwood that her jealousy has indeed turned to hate. We are, as readers, given to understand that she enjoys the prospect of running the household and the family affairs without Hurstwood's presence, and that she intends to press her advantage by hiring a lawyer and a detective. Her first large gesture is to send a messenger demanding the money she requires from Hurstwood, after he has spent the night away from home, in a hotel. Upon receiving a second note, Hurstwood resolves to take the money to her and have things out. Thus he finds himself locked out of his own house, the locks having been changed in his day's absence.

Comment

This and the ensuing chapters which deal with the cold, detached (and such rapid-fire) actions on the part of Mrs. Hurstwood tend to tax the reader's credulity. The absolute and irrevocable quality of what happens in the following pages, through, let us say, Hurstwood's thievery at the club, is perhaps but scantily prevented from becoming "melodrama" by the fast pace of the action. The question to be raised is whether or not we have been sufficiently prepared as readers for the abrupt and impulsive actions of both Mr. and Mrs. Hurstwood in this crisis.

CHAPTER 25: ASHES OF TINDER: THE LOOSING OF STAYS

This chapter is more of the same - that is, of the rapid disintegration of Hurstwood's superficially ordered existence and his own resulting confusions when put on the defensive. We should recall, however, that he has previously understood his wife's capacity for outraged vanity and calculated restitution for wrongs. He sends her the requested money, but on Monday he finds himself addressed by mail from the law offices of McGregor, James and Hay on behalf of Mrs. Hurstwood. This note, ignored helplessly by Hurstwood, is followed upon on Wednesday by one informing him that if he is not heard from by the following day, action will be taken on his wife's behalf for divorce and alimony. (The reader will recall that part of Hurstwood's dilemma is that in the early, rosier days of his matrimonial alliance he had put much of his real estate in his wife's name.)

Comment

The sensible reader is bound to inquire at this point why in the world Hurstwood doesn't get his own lawyer and fight. The answer, possibly weak, seems to be that he is confused by his rapidly crashing world around him, wherein he had supposed himself the authoritarian, just out to add a little extra pleasure to his slim quota. He is also held back by his guilty association with Carrie, assuming, as do all people with any guilty items on their conscience, that his wife possesses a good deal more real information than she does. In addition, he is still driven by his desires for the girl.

CHAPTER 26: THE AMBASSADOR FALLEN: A SEARCH FOR THE GATE

Carrie is now confronted with her aloneness, Drouet having stormed out. (We as readers suspect that he intends to return and make up, but Carrie in her confusion does not realize this.) "To her credit, be it said, she never once counted on Hurstwood. She could only approach that subject with a pang of sorrow and regret. For a truth, she was rather shocked and frightened by this evidence of human depravity. He would have tricked her without turning an eyelash. She would have been led into a newer and worse situation. And yet she could not keep out the pictures of his looks and manners. Only this one deed seemed strange and miserable. It contrasted sharply with all she felt and knew concerning the man." However Dreiser may disparage Carrie's powers of mind and ultimate logic, what he depicts here is a real conflict. Her reflections at this moment contain the truth of human conflict, which is indeed the very inevitability of the conflicting interests and facts. The validity of her response cannot be denied. She realizes she is alone, and that she must eventually make motions to find a job and earn some money.

"She could not help feeling, as she looked across the lovely park, that life was a joyous thing for those who did not need to worry, and she wished over and over that something might interfere now to preserve for her the comfortable state which she had occupied. She did not want Drouet or his money when she thought of it, nor anything more to do with Hurstwood, but only the content and ease of mind she had experienced, for, after all, she had been happy-happier at least, than she was now when confronted by the necessity of making her way alone." It is perhaps Carrie's first real confrontation of the long-range consequences of her actions, and it is, again, an honest response, realistic and uncolored by any false moralizing by the author.

It is rather inevitable that she should turn in her job-hunting to the theatre-ineffectively in her ignorance of its operations. It is also inevitable that, having made a few attempts, her spirits will be "materially reduced, owing to the newly restored sense of magnitude of the great interests and the insignificance of her claims upon society, such as she understood them to be." And it is ironic that in her timid, abortive little job-hunting venture, she misses Drouet's return to the flat for some of his things. He had returned, obviously, to make things up with her, but again chance and circumstance determine destiny. Finding her out (where he knows not and can too well imagine), he at length leaves, more decisively than the first time.

CHAPTER 27: WHEN WATERS ENGULF US WE REACH FOR A STAR

Again, as chance and circumstances will have it, Hurstwood, returning from a disturbed stroll after receiving the decisive note from Mrs. Hurstwood's lawyers, finds a letter from Carrie. It says, in one of her more affirmative tones, that she is shocked by his deception and will not see him again. Yet, in spite of the contents, this letter is to Hurstwood the "one resource against the depression which held him." He tells himself that she would not write at all if she did not love him. Dreiser describes it sensitively: "There was really something exceedingly human-if not pathetic-in his being thus relieved by a clearly worded reproof. He who had for so long remained satisfied with himself now looked outside of himself for comfort - and to such a source. The mystic cords of affection! How they bind us all." (This bond is paralleled by the correspondingly inexplicable one which Carrie will shortly be made to feel toward Hurstwood when they meet again.)

The passages which deal with Hurstwood's mental fluctuation and conflict when, upon doing his habitual nightly checkup of the receipts, etc., he finds the safe incredibly unlocked, are among the most brilliant in the novel. Dreiser traces, with the acumen of one who perceives the nuances of the workings of the human mind, point for point the process whereby Hurstwood at last finds himself, definitively and disastrously, still in reluctant possession of the ten thousand dollars. As Dreiser perfectly observes, "At every first adventure, then, into some untried evil, the mind wavers. The clock of thought ticks out its wish and its denial." The author also realizes that "to those who have never wavered in conscience, the predicament of the individual whose mind is less strongly constituted and who trembles in the balance between duty and desire is scarcely appreciable, unless graphically portrayed." What follows of course is just such a graphic portrayal. But in the end the final decision still rests on a fluke: while Hurstwood indecisively holds the money in his hand, the lock clicks shut and he is left with the money damagingly outside of the safe. From here on, he acts upon the half-thinking impulses of the fleeing fugitive. He arranges for his flight, intending to abduct Carrie as well.

CHAPTER 28: A PILGRIM, AN OUTLAW: THE SPIRIT DETAINED

There is now, of course, no limit to Hurstwood's deception, given the will to thrust through his necessary course of action. He unhesitatingly enlists Carrie's companionship by informing her that Drouet has been injured. In this manner she accompanies him, though more and more curiously as the train goes on. Hurstwood's mental state is bitter. "In his sober senses, he could scarcely realize that the thing had been done. He could not begin to feel that he was a fugitive from justice... . His condition was bitter in the extreme, for he did not want the miserable sum he had stolen. He did not want to be a thief. That sum or any other could never compensate for the state which he had thus foolishly doffed. It could not give him back his host of friends, his name, his house and family, nor Carrie, as he had meant to have her. He was shut out from Chicago-from his easy comfortable state. He had robbed himself of his dignity, his merry meetings, his pleasant evenings. And for what? The more he thought of it the more unbearable it became." Here again, the **realism** of Hurstwood's state-the very humanness of it-evokes pathos. The passage is both an astute summary of his present condition, and a grim **foreshadowing** of his future.

Carrie, as we might expect, is at first vehement in her protest against his further dishonesty toward her; but at length she is ineffectual to halt the course of her own destiny, intertwining with Hurstwood's more and more as the wheels of the train roll round and round away from Chicago. Although she verbalizes her thought of leaving the train at the next stop, she remains with Hurstwood, in their dreamy nightmare ride which will come to rest at last in Montreal.

CHAPTER 29: THE SOLACE OF TRAVEL: THE BOATS OF THE SEA

While Carrie is able-true to herself-to dissipate undertones of anxiety by the sheer novelty of travel and arriving in a new place, Hurstwood's tension in Montreal is relaxed but little. Upon coming downstairs in the hotel he comes upon a Chicago friend, who obviously has not read the papers. Furthermore, as he returns to his rooms, he notes a person who looks very much like a detective and who, indeed, knocks on their hotel room door shortly. To this privately hired representative of Hurstwood's firm he asserts that he has made up his mind and has written Fitzgerald and Moy, etc. This in effect is what he subsequently does, offering to undo the major portion of his crime by sending most of the money back, the remainder to be paid back little by little. He also hints at the possibility of being restored to his former place. But the author puts Hurstwood's position more bluntly: "The troubled state of the man's mind may be judged by the very construction of this letter. For the once he forgot what a painful thing it would be to resume his old place, even if it were given him. He forgot that he had severed himself from the past as by a sword, and that if he did manage to in some way reunite himself with it, the jagged line of separation and reunion would always show. He was always forgetting something-his wife, Carrie, his need of money, present situation or something - and so did not reason clearly." The reply from his employers is an acceptance of his terms.

Meanwhile Hurstwood's need for Carrie is now great: he looks at her "with love now keen and strong-love enhanced by difficulty and worry." Carrie accepts his proposals "solemnly. There was no great passion in her, but the drift of things and this man's proximity created a semblance of affection. She felt rather sorry for him-a sorrow born of what had only recently been a great admiration. True love she had never felt for him. She would have known as much if she could have analyzed her feelings, but this thing which she now felt aroused by his great feeling broke down the barriers between them." They are married by a Baptist minister before their departure for New York.

New York, of course, is quite another thing from Chicago's open space. Upon their arrival Carrie, observing tall five-story buildings everywhere, ask where the residential section is. "Everywhere," said Hurstwood, who knew the city fairly well. "There are no lawns in New York. All these are houses." "Well, then, I don't like it" said Carrie, who was coming to have a few opinions of her own.

Comment

Do not miss the **irony**, rather frequent, of Dreiser's chapter titles: i.e., "The Solace of Travel" (Carrie's ability to escape from the "real" world of problems and decisions); "When Waters Engulf Us We Reach for a Star" (Hurstwood, as he sinks in confusions and complications, impulsively steals).

CHAPTER 30: THE KINGDOM OF GREATNESS: THE PILGRIM, A DREAM

In this chapter is suggested the contrast between Chicago and New York and Hurstwood's realization of his changed status. Contrary to Chicago, where "the two roads to distinction were politics and trade," in New York there were many modes of success: here Hurstwood is the proverbial little fish in a big big pond. Dreiser makes his descriptive point well, **foreshadowing** the creeping realities of Hurstwood's situation: "There is a more subtle result of such a situation as this, which, though not always taken into account, produces the tragedies of the world. The great create an atmosphere which reacts badly upon the small. This atmosphere is easily and quickly felt. Walk among the magnificent residences, the splendid equipages, the gilded shops, restaurants, resorts of all kinds; ... feel the quality of the smiles which cut like glistening swords and of strides born of place and you shall know of what is the atmosphere of the high and mighty. Little use to argue that of such is not the kingdom of greatness, but so long as the world is attracted by this and the human heart views this as the one desirable realm which it must attain, so long, to that heart, will this remain the realm of greatness. So long, also, will the atmosphere of this realm work its desperate results in the soul of man." The remainder of the novel is really about just these desperate results. Even Carrie's "success" is born of the same desperation, and is, at last, discontented. Hurstwood realizes that here in New York is "gathered all that he most respected on this earth-wealth, place, and fame." At the same time, facing this city, he himself is "cut off from his friends, despoiled of his modest fortune and even his name and forced to begin the battle for place and comfort all over again."

At the same time, their changed condition (although she is not aware of Hurstwood's theft), economically and socially, comes to Carrie little by little. Even the very secretiveness with which Hurstwood attempts to conceal his tight financial situation works on Carrie's imagination-she is not in his confidence. "She found herself asking him questions about little things. This is a disagreeable state to a woman. Great love makes it seem reasonable, sometimes plausible, but never satisfactory. Where great love is not, a more definite and less satisfactory conclusion is reached." Dreiser is telling us that in the best of relationships the frailties of human nature will from time to time strain a matrimonial union: "Little things brought out on such occasions need great love to obliterate them afterward. Where that is not, both parties count two and two and make a problem after a while." Thus as readers we expect, and wait for, the "problem."

CHAPTER 31: A PET OF GOOD FORTUNE: BROADWAY FLAUNTS ITS JOYS

Dreiser here portrays the process by which Carrie's desires for pleasure are re-aroused. Again, her conflicts depicted by the end of this chapter result from the creeping changes of circumstance, and the corresponding altered response in people, especially Hurstwood. At first, in New York, Carrie is somewhat content to develop in domesticity; also, Hurstwood, grateful for her presence, is devotedly affectionate. By the second year however, his financial strain has eased somewhat: "Unfortunately, by this time Carrie had reached certain conclusions, and he had scraped up a few acquaintances." Hurstwood in short makes the error of supposing that Carrie is at heart a simple, domestic type; he begins to contribute only what he sees as part of these satisfactions to her. Thus she begins to feel his neglect. He "naturally abandoned his show of fine manners with her and modified his attitude to one of easy familiarity. There were no misunderstandings, no apparent differences of opinion." This is perhaps because Carrie is "passive and receptive" rather than "active and aggressive."

But as circumstance will always have it (in a Dreiser novel at least), Carrie's neighbor Mrs. Vance enters the picture at this point, and with her Carrie is thus introduced to the New York social whirl she has been unaware of. Walking down Broadway with the well-dressed Mrs. Vance clears up Carrie's vague ideas of discontent and depression: "She could only imagine that it must be evident to many that she was the less handsomely dressed of the two. It cut her to the quick, and she resolved that she would not come here again until she looked better. At the same time she longed to feel the delight of parading here as an equal. Ah, then she would be happy!" We recall that the one issue on which the former more timid Carrie would express herself (to her brother-in-law) was the assertion of her desire for pleasure. The desire and the conflict (as is often the case with the "plateaus" of existence) have merely been dormant.

CHAPTER 32: THE FEAST OF BELSHAZZAR: A SEER TO TRANSLATE

At the matinee she attends with Mrs. Vance, the vivid lure of the theatre is once more imposed upon Carrie's imagination. She has never forgotten her first theatrical achievement. Dreiser comments with gentle **irony** upon the "drawing-room concoction in which charmingly overdressed ladies and gentlemen suffer the pangs of love and jealousy amid gilded surroundings." He thus indicates how that present society he writes about would have been inclined to seek out this make-believe world which also emphasizes appearance over reality. The "cheat" of such drama is revealed in the author's remarks. "They have the charm of showing suffering under ideal conditions. Who would not grieve upon a gilded chair? Who would not suffer amid perfumed tapestries, cushioned furniture, and liveried servants? Grief under such circumstances becomes an enticing thing. Carrie longed to be of it. She wanted to take her sufferings, whatever they were, in such a world, or failing that, at least to simulate to be of it. She wanted to take her sufferings whatever they were, in such a world, or failing that, at least to simulate them under such charming conditions upon the stage." Carrie is indeed "lost" in a very fated sense in this sort of world.

Another aspect is added by Dr. Iser to his vast panorama of American society in the 1900s: the dining **episode** at Sherry's, where Mr. Vance is in his element just as Hurstwood would have once been in Chicago. "Once seated, there begun that exhibition of showy, wasteful, and unwholesome gastronomy as practiced by wealthy Americans, which is the wonder and astonishment of true culture and dignity the world over. The large bill of fare held an array of dishes sufficient to feed an army, sidelined with prices which made reasonable expenditure a ridiculous impossibility... ."

The one seeming reality in the midst of all this fantastic appearance of material well-being is the figure of Mr. Ames, the cousin who has accompanied them to Sherry's. He strikes Carrie-rightly-as another type of man from any she has ever been exposed to. From his comments on the scene around them she senses that he is educated, and thoughtful about life. "The saving grace in Carrie was that she could understand that people could be wiser." Although he may sound to the reader very much like the first-year graduate student of literature in his offhand dismissals when the conversation turns to some current fiction, yet in one sense Carrie's impression of him is accurate: he is the most reflective man she has ever encountered. She realizes that the book spoken of "was poor to him, not worth reading. She looked down, and for the first time felt the pain of not understanding."

Comment

The introduction of Mr. Ames, and what he stands for, albeit modestly, is quite significant. It is strongly suggested here, when Ames attempts to influence Carrie in her theatrical career toward more serious drama, that he is a human being several rungs up on that ladder toward reason and the exercise of free will, as opposed to all creatures we have thus far met in the novel, each in his own way a wisp in the wind, driven (and but faintly aware of it) by deterministic forces.

Thus the conclusion to the chapter is worth noting also: "Back in the dining room she sat in her chair and rocked. Her little hands were folded tightly as she thought. Through a fog of longing and conflicting desires she was beginning to see. Oh. ye legions of hope and pity-of sorrow and pain! She was rocking, and beginning to see." The question is, then, how much will Carrie ever really see, and how much will she be left in the end, with "the pain of not understanding." The rocking chair, as we will see more and more, at least approaches being a symbol. It is a representation of Carrie's wishful, even intense desires, of her yet ultimately ineffectual realization of what is real happiness, the deeper sort of content that Mr. Ames seems to stand for.

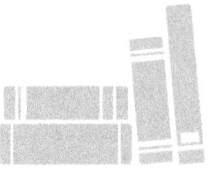

SISTER CARRIE

TEXTUAL ANALYSIS

CHAPTERS 33–47

CHAPTER 33: WITHOUT THE WALLED CITY: THE SLOPE OF THE YEARS

The "slope of the years" suggests, of course, the downward path, psychologically, for Hurstwood after his Chicago fiasco and his entrance into the bar partnership in New York City. The changes that subtly but inevitably occur in Hurstwood naturally have their corresponding effect on Carrie's attitudes toward him. This chapter strongly intimates the downhill way which will lead, at last, to the Bowery. "Not trained to reason or introspect himself, he could not analyze the change that was taking place in his mind, and hence his body, but he felt the depression of it. Constant comparisons between his old state and his new showed a balance for the worse, which produced a constant state of gloom or, at least depression." Thus Hurstwood begins to understand that he himself is now excluded more and more from this "city with a wall about it," the city of ample raiment and money to spend.

As for Carrie, to Hurstwood's confession that the business is doing poorly, that economies must be practiced, "her reply was mild enough, but her thoughts were rebellious." Thus the eventual move to a cheaper flat "affected her more seriously than anything that had yet happened. She began to look upon Hurstwood wholly as a man, and not as a lover or husband." Life looks more and more like a "dull round."

Comment

Dreiser's continuing care to maintain a psychological **realism** toward his characters is indicated in the following passage. "If one thinks that such thoughts [i.e. Hurstwood's frustrated awareness of his exclusion from the walled wealth of New York] do not come to so common a type of mind-that such feelings require a higher mental development-I would urge for their consideration the fact that it is the higher mental development that does away with such thoughts. It is the higher mental development which induces philosophy and that fortitude which refuses to dwell upon such things-refuses to be made to suffer by their consideration. The common type of mind is exceedingly keen on all matters which relate to its physical welfare-exceedingly keen. It is the unintellectual miser who sweats blood at the loss of a hundred dollars." The italics I have added here call attention once more to Dreiser's insistence on the preconditioned compulsions toward material things in his characters.

CHAPTER 34: THE GRIND OF THE MILLSTONES: A SAMPLE OF CHAFF

Dreiser handles the growing alienation between Hurstwood and Carrie with pathos, **irony**, and, as usual, nonjudgment. As

Hurstwood is faced with the closing of his bar and the termination of his partnership with Shaughnessy, Carrie's thoughts revolve around many things: remembrance of the grimness of Hanson-type poverty in Chicago, as well as of her dismal experiment with working there; her recent exposure to the glamour of New York, coupled with her own development into a woman of taste, which calls for ample means. Superimposed on these reflections in Carrie is the "ideal brought into her life by Ames....He had gone, but here was his word that riches were not everything; that there was a great deal more in the world than she knew; that the stage was good, and the literature she read poor."

Although Hurstwood makes feeble attempts to find a new situation, the closing day of his bar finds him without future arrangements for employment - and with savings of $700. Dreiser returns to the effective symbolism of the rocking chair to suggest the fateful apathy which now sets in on Hurstwood. "He buried himself in his papers and read. Oh, the rest of it - the relief from walking and thinking! What Lethean waters were these floods of telegraphed intelligence! He forgot his troubles, in part. Here was a young, handsome woman, if you might believe the newspaper drawing, suing a rich fat, candy-making husband in Brooklyn for divorce. Here was another item detailing the wrecking of a vessel in ice and snow off Prince's Bay on Staten Island... . So he read, read, read, rocking in the warm room near the radiator and waiting for dinner to be served."

CHAPTER 35: THE PASSING OF EFFORT: THE VISAGE OF CARE

The insidious process by which Hurstwood will at length join the ranks of unemployed men is realistically and humanly detailed from here on. Well-dressed as he still at this point, when he walks into places of business seeking second-rate positions, his executive look actually works against him; nor can he very realistically imagine himself in the very positions he is forced to apply for. So he takes lots of time out from job-hunting to eat lunch, and later, to rest in the lobby of a great hotel. When the winter weather takes a turn for the worse, he convinces himself he needn't go out searching on such a bad day. And, for the first time (but by no means the last), he suggests doing a household errand for Carrie, although "he really thought nothing of these little services in connection with their true significance. He felt as if he were not wholly useless-indeed, in such a stress of weather, quite worth-while about the house." The poisonous process of apathy toward a terrifying outside world, and rationalization toward his own state, will inevitably destroy his self-image. And, "of course, as his own self-respect vanished it perished for him in Carrie… . She did not forget her own difficult struggle in Chicago, but she did not forget either that she had never ceased trying." Carrie begins to sleep alone.

CHAPTER 36: A GRIM RETROGRESSION: THE PHANTOM OF CHANCE

This is a chapter of reversals and revelations. Hurstwood in foolish desperation turns to gambling, and loses. As he and Carrie increasingly bicker, he is driven to reveal to her that he didn't actually marry her back in Montreal. The more Hurstwood realizes that he has treated Carrie badly in certain respects and yet that he cannot "afford to make up" with her, the more he hastens his own destruction by wandering out each day and living it up like a gentleman. The chapter concludes with his bitter return, on rent day, to the reality he is down to his last hundred dollars.

CHAPTER 37: THE SPIRIT AWAKENS: NEW SEARCH FOR THE GATE

Here we find a short account of Carrie's reawakened interest in the stage, faced as she is with Hurstwood's inability to continue the search for employment. Aware in a way that to encourage her in this revitalized interest is to contribute somehow to his own doom, Hurstwood yet sends her out to look for theatrical employment. He "saw her depart with some faint stirrings of shame, which were the expression of a manhood rapidly becoming stultified. He sat awhile, and then it became too much. He got up and put on his hat." His life has become a series of alternate escapisms between rocking and walking, aimlessly.

Comment

There is one passage in this chapter which we might well reserve for future reference. When it occurs to Carrie to return to the theatre, Hurstwood's ideas run like this: "In a flash, he thought he foresaw the result of this thing. Now, when the worst of his situation was approaching, she would get on the stage in some cheap way and forsake him. Strangely, he had not conceived well of her mental ability. That was because he did not understand the nature of emotional greatness. He had never learned that a person might be emotionally-instead of intellectually-great." The main idea here seems to be that, as the author states, someone like Carrie could be "emotionally" instead of "intellectually" great. The inference, which turns out to be true, is that such ability might very well lead her to the stage, not in a cheap but in an elevated way.

CHAPTER 38: IN ELF LAND DISPORTING: THE GRIM WORLD WITHOUT

Although Carrie's early rounds of the theatres are inefficient and dispiriting, at last she secures interview with the manager of the Casino and subsequently is given a place among the chorus girls there. Her momentary elation about the job, with its twelve dollars a week, is soon tempered by her realization that such news may increase Hurstwood's apathy, which indeed it does. By now Hurstwood has become a chronic liar with respect to his job-hunting and job prospects; and the fact of Carrie's twelve dollars per week is enough to prompt him to make the final plunge, asking her to "help" him financially, until he gets a place.

CHAPTER 39: OF LIGHTS AND OF SHADOWS: THE PARTING OF WORLDS

This chapter crucially focuses on the deciding conflicts of the final third of the novel. Carrie finds herself reluctantly supporting the household while Hurstwood takes over all the chores of shopping (and of putting off the payment of bills to the local shopkeepers). At the same time her old love of pretty adornment and pleasure is reawakened by comparison to the girls she works with at the Casino: "Her need of clothes-to say nothing of her desire for ornaments-grew rapidly as the fact developed that for all her work she was not to have them." Yet we have to note that Carrie is not hardened or vicious toward Hurstwood, as we witness her reflections upon his expenditure of her earnings: "Hurstwood bought the flour-which all grocers sold in 3 1/2-pound packages-for thirteen cents and paid fifteen cents for a half-pound of liver and bacon. He left the packages, together with the balance of twenty-two cents, upon the kitchen table, where Carrie found it. It did not escape her that the change was accurate. There was something sad in realizing that, after all, all that he wanted of her was something to eat. She felt as if hard thoughts were unjust. Maybe he would get something yet. He had no vices." It is a passage terrible in pathos and **irony**, for it draws the reader into the hopeless dilemma of these two characters whose lives are now fatally destined to go in opposite directions, not because they are mean and vicious people-perhaps because they are weak and indecisive people - but certainly because they remain to the end queerly unaware and innocent of the circumstances which contrive against them, whether external or from inside themselves. The passage, however, is especially horrifying in its ruthless, but quite realistic, depiction of how a man slowly but surely becomes less than a man.

Since at the Casino in her dancing "she did unconsciously move about with an air pleasing and somewhat distinctive.. due wholly to her natural manner and total lack of self-consciousness," Carrie begins to feel both more successful and more independent, spending time, for example, with her pleasing young colleague, Miss Osborne. And Hurstwood questions, but passively, her increasing absence: he "saw it all clearly enough. He was shrewd after his kind, and yet there was enough decency in the man to stop him from making any effectual protest. In his almost inexplicable apathy he was content to droop supinely while Carrie drifted out of his life, just as he was willing supinely to see opportunity pass beyond his control. He could not help clinging and protesting in a mild, irritating, and ineffectual way, however-a way that simply widened the breach by slow degrees."

CHAPTER 40: A PUBLIC DISSENSION: A FINAL APPEAL

Another crisis develops here. Carrie increasingly realizes that Hurstwood is sinking, that he has no intention of getting employment, and finally, that he has been holding off on the grocer's bill, so that this personage is obliged to confront them personally at their flat for his money. The "hotel" to be opened by a "Mr. Drake," is of course mythical, so that Carrie's inquiry about it is met by "Yes. He won't do it before October, though, now." And she is "aware" of the subterfuge to the extent that she gradually becomes "disgusted. 'Such a man,' she said to herself frequently. More and more she visited. She put most of her spare money in clothes, which, after all, was not an astonishing amount." When thus confronted with various unpaid bills for their household expenses, Carrie puts her foot down and says she cannot handle all their support.

It is at this point that Hurstwood, "sick of the grind of this thing," pays more attention to rumors of a strike on the Brooklyn trolley lines. What ensues is, really, the last point in the novel in which we can consider Hurstwood in a truly admirable light: he answers the advertisement for motormen and conductors to replace those who are striking. Carrie's conversation with him prior to his attempt is telling: "'Aren't you afraid?' she asked." He replies that police protection is being provided (protection, as we later learn, which is rather sympathetic to the striking men). "Yes,' he returned; 'but you can't go by what the papers say. They'll run the cars all right.' He looked rather determined now, in a desolate sort of way, and Carrie felt very sorry. Something of the old Hurstwood was here-the least shadow of what was once shrewd and pleasant strength. Outside it was cloudy and blowing a few flakes of snow. 'What a day to go over there', thought Carrie. Now he left before she did, which was a remarkable thing… ."

Comment

The reader is to be reminded here that, in addition to Dreiser's portrayal of Hurstwood's really final gesture toward remaining a "man," there is the grueling picture of working conditions in general in the 1900s, and of "labor's little wars," which were, of course, to increase with success in our century. Hurstwood, in short, becomes for the moment a "scab," ordinarily a hated, derogatory term. Yet, we as readers who know Hurstwood and his personal situation, manage (as I believe is Dreiser's intent) to sympathize both with the social ill and the personal disaster of a man.

CHAPTER 41: THE STRIKE

This is more a description of the strike - and the conditions which prompted it-than it is a narration of Hurstwood's passive, almost dreamy participation in the employer's attempt to run the cars. Hurstwood observes, at the barn where he reports in Brooklyn, "a lot of green hands around-queer, hungry-looking men, who looked as if want had driven them to desperate means. They tried to be lively and willing but there was an air of hangdog diffidence about the place." It is natural, yet heavily ironic, that he excludes himself from their condition and conversation. One man remarks "It's hell these days, ain't it? A poor man ain't nowhere. You could starve, by God, right in the streets, and there ain't most no one would help you." Another man answers, "Right you are. The job I had I lost 'cause they shut down. They run all summer and lay up a big stock and then shut down."

As suggested, Dreiser is making two chief points here: one involves his conviction (which was quite justified) that it was "hell" those days for the poor; the other point of course is his heavily ironic finger laid upon the dark shadow of Hurstwood's imminent fate. Yet, to the above conversation, "Hurstwood paid some little attention.... Somehow, he felt a little superior to these two-a little better off. To him these were ignorant and commonplace, poor sheep in a driver's hand. 'Poor devils,' he thought, speaking out of the thoughts and feelings of a bygone period of success." The first afternoon he merely trains with a car, without taking one out. Faced with the need for a place to sleep, and for food (for return to New York is impossible), he finds that there are cots available in a loft, for such as him. "He ate in a cheap restaurant in the vicinity, and, being cold and lonely, went straight off to seek the loft in question. The company was not attempting to run cars after nightfall. It was so advised by the police." The uneasy sleep in the dirty bed along with the meal ticket he is obliged to ask for the next morning, although he does not know it, grimly foreshadow his future state.

Dreiser conveys the misery of the whole situation by simply telling the facts: "There was no water on this floor. He put on his shoes in the cold and stood up, shaking himself in his stiffness. His clothes felt disagreeable, his hair bad.... He found a hydrant, with a trough which had once been used for horses, but there was no towel here, and his handkerchief was soiled from yesterday." The description of Hurstwood's trip out and back with a car, accompanied by two policemen, is similarly treated: all the jeers, the hatred, the actual violence (and obstruction of the trolley tracks) that have proverbially awaited the strike-breaker or "scab" confront Hurstwood. Although he is driven for a time by his last remnant of desire to prove Carrie that he can do something after all, when his day of chaos and destruction is capped by a pistol shot which stings past his shoulder, Hurstwood finally steps down and makes his way home, in a snowstorm. In the ferry, the "cabins were filled with comfortable souls, who studied him curiously. His head was still in such a whirl that he felt confused... . He trudged doggedly on until he reached the flat. There he entered and found the room warm. Carrie was gone. A couple of evening papers were lying on the table where she left them. He lit the gas and sat down... . He washed his hands and face, still in a brown study, apparently, and combed his hair. Then he looked for something to eat, and finally, his hunger gone, sat down in his comfortable rocking chair. It was a wonderful relief." Hurstwood is back in the rocking chair reading the paper, absorbing with intense interest the news of the strike and the riots. This is where he will now remain, until his condition still further deteriorates.

CHAPTER 42: A TOUCH OF SPRING: THE EMPTY SHELL

"Those who look upon Hurstwood's Brooklyn venture as an error of judgment will none the less realize the negative influence on him of the fact that he had tried and failed. Carrie got a wrong idea of it. He said so little that she imagined he had encountered nothing worse than the ordinary roughness-quitting so soon in the face of this seemed trifling. He did not want to work." Beginning with this added **irony** of Hurstwood's further victimization by circumstance, we move on immediately to Carrie's "chance" success on stage one evening, when she wittily replies to an unexpected question by the star comedian. The audience laughs; and when the audience laughs, the lines stay in. Thus Carrie's present conflict revolves around her increasing success and frustration at economic burdens, the pressure from her little friend Miss Osborne (who does not realize she is "married") to join her in sharing a room on 17th Street, and her observation of Hurstwood's growing passivity. But, "each day looking at Hurstwood, she had realized that, along with the disagreeableness of his attitude, there was something pathetic." She feels most guilty, naturally enough, on the day she intends at last to actually move out and go with Miss Osborne. She pulls out a two-dollar bill and urges him to get something nice for dinner: "Hurstwood rose and took the money, slipping on his overcoat and getting his hat. Carrie noticed that both of these articles of apparel were old and poor-looking in appearance. It was plain enough before, but now it came home with peculiar force. Perhaps he couldn't help it, after all. He had done well in Chicago. She remembered his fine appearance the days he had met her in the park. Then he was so sprightly, so clean. Had it been all his fault? The question is posed both by Carrie - and it is perhaps the nearest she, or any of the other characters in Dreiser's novel, gets to an "awareness" of the forces which shape destinies - and in a general way by the author to the reader; for it involves his entire thesis: whose fault was it, the fate of these people?

As Carrie contemplates her final severance from Hurstwood, it is natural that her thoughts would return to the separation from Drouet, about which she feels guilty, yet, as always, confused as to the motives for guilt. The motives are far more complex than she could ever comprehend. "She had looked back at times upon her parting from Drouet and had regretted that she had served him so badly. She hoped she would never meet him again, but she was ashamed of her conduct. Not that she had any choice in the final separation. She had gone willingly to seek him, with sympathy in her heart, when Hurstwood had reported him ill. There was something cruel somewhere, and not being able to track it mentally to its logical lair, she concluded with feeling that he would never understand what Hurstwood had done and would see hardhearted decision in her deed; hence her shame. Not that she cared for him. She did not want to make anyone who had been good to her feel badly." These feelings thus are paralleled by her current emotions upon leaving Hurstwood. Carrie is as good-natured as was Drouet, but she is a drifter in the confusions of her own world, and in the end she is as "lost" as Hurstwood. The most significant point made here is that there is, indeed, "something cruel somewhere."

The remaining passages of the chapter, which describe Hurstwood's return to the flat deserted by Carrie, pull very strongly upon the reader. Again, all that Dreiser needs to do in order to enlist the reader's acute sympathy is to describe the simple actions and reactions of any man confronted with a similar situation. Hurstwood discovers gradually that her favorite things and her belongings are gone; he finds himself holding the twenty dollars she has left; and, at last, he realizes his lonely state. "The place that had been so comfortable, where he had spent so many days of warmth, was now a memory. Something colder and chillier confronted him. He sank down in his chair, resting his chin in his hand - mere sensation, without thought, holding him. Then something like a bereaved affection and self-pity swept over him. 'She needn't have gone away,' he said. 'I'd have got something.' He sat a long while without rocking, and added quite clearly, out loud: 'I tried, didn't I?' At midnight he was still rocking, staring at the floor."

Comment

One of the secrets of Carrie's ultimate theatrical success is buried, as rather incidental to the mainstream of the action, in this chapter. The author remarks that, "timid as Carrie was, she was strong in capability. The reliance of others made her feel as if she must, and when she must she dared. Experience of the world and of necessity was in her favor. No longer the lightest word of a man made her head dizzy. She had learned that men could change and fail. Flattery in its most palpable form had lost its force with her." In the remaining chapters we will see more and more of this force of independence in her; but unfortunately, it is this very same "experience" of life which will also isolate her, in the end, from fellow humans and from real contentment.

CHAPTER 43: THE WORLD TURNS FLATTERER: AN EYE IN THE DARK

Here the public world does indeed turn flatterer, and boosts Carrie on her flight upward from small notices in the theatrical pages, with her thirty-five dollars a week, to her ultimate triumph as the frowning Quaker maid. Instantaneous public success easily convinces the manager that he had better buy her quickly at one hundred fifty per week. Yet Carrie's only friend is Miss Osborne; there is nobody, she discovers, to whom she would like to send notices of her success. Furthermore, there is the undiscriminating coldness of the city, making little distinction in its real gestures of friendship between a Carrie and a Hurstwood: "The metropolis is a cold place socially, and Carrie soon found that a little money brought her nothing... . She could feel that there was no warm, sympathetic friendship back of the easy merriment with which many approached her. All seemed to be seeking their own amusement, regardless of the possible sad consequence to others. So much for the lessons of Hurstwood and Drouet."

Meanwhile Dreiser does not forego the pathetic contrast- probably approaching sentimentality, even melodrama-of

Hurstwood's condition upon discovering Carrie's success. He is in a third-rate Bleecker Street hotel, reading of her triumph in a "dingy, moth-eaten hotel lobby." "'I guess she's struck it,' he thought, a picture of the old shiny, plush-covered world coming back, with its lights, its ornaments, its carriages, and flowers. Ah, she was in the walled city now! Its splendid gates had opened, admitting her from a cold, dreary outside. She seemed a creature afar off-like every other celebrity he had known. 'Well, let her have it,' he said. 'I won't bother her.' It was the grim resolution of a bent, bedraggled, but unbroken pride."

CHAPTER 44: AND THIS IS NOT ELF LAND: WHAT GOLD WILL NOT BUY

This chapter is simply true to its title; it deals with Carrie's adulation, her feelings about it, and her discoveries of what money will not buy. At the theatre, "she was no longer ordered, but requested, and that politely." Yet she retains an innate modesty instead of developing a manner of the star: "When her associates addressed her in the wings she only smiled weakly. The pride and daring of place were not for her. It never once crossed her mind to be reserved or haughty-to be other than she had been." It is then just another stage in her flight upward that she is invited by a representative to take up residence at the Wellington, for the prestige which her reputation will lend to the establishment! The gentleman assures her, "You need not trouble with terms. In fact, we need hardly discuss them."

Her encounter with Mrs. Vance - whom she has not seen since that lady's embarrassed confrontation of the bearded, ill-kempt Hurstwood at their flat months ago - is in a similar vein of contrast between her old and her new worlds: "It came to her that she was as good as this woman now - perhaps better.

Something in the other's solicitude and interest made her feel as if she were the one to condescend." Carrie is a public figure; she is installed in luxurious quarters, the daily recipient of letters and calls of adulation from admirers. Yet the chapter closes on a somber note. "It does not take money long to make plain its impotence, providing the desires are in the realm of affection." Carrie is without friends, with nothing to do. She listens to her vivacious, untroubled friend, Lola Osborne, exhorting her to get out and enjoy herself; she watches the passing crowd down on Broadway. "Unconsciously her idle hands were beginning to weary."

CHAPTER 45: CURIOUS SHIFTS OF THE POOR

Here again Dreiser is driven by dual intentions: to portray Hurstwood's personal tragedy, and to etch memorably on the reader's mind the public disaster of poverty in New York of the 1900s (and, unfortunately, in any area where poverty exists in any period). Hurstwood's downward trek from fifty cents to thirty-five cents to fifteen cents for a room, this time on the Bowery, is inevitable. The lodging house in the Bowery has a "bare lounging room filled with tables and benches as well as some chairs. Here his preference was to close his eyes and dream of other days, a habit which grew upon him. It was not sleep at first, but a mental hearkening back to scenes and incidents in his Chicago life. As the present became darker, the past grew brighter, and all that concerned it stood out in relief."

When his money finally runs out (he had sold the furniture from the flat), he summons all his courage and walks into the Broadway Central hotel. This is the very place where he would have met his Chicago friends once, and, later, where he used to lounge on the futile job-hunting ventures. Now, he asks for something to do. Down-and-out as he is and looks he is yet curiously driven to relate to the comfortable manager of the hotel the incredible tale of his own past career as a manager: incredible because the "figure of Hurstwood was rather surprising in contrast to the fact." The manager inquires how he came to get out of that line of business. "Well, by foolishness of my own. It isn't anything to talk about now. You could find out if you wanted to. I'm broke now and, if you will believe me, I haven't eaten anything today." Having aroused a mild interest in the manager, Hurstwood is given a place at the hotel, where he manages to work and survive for a while. "With the stolidity and indifference of despair, however, he endured it all sleeping in an attic at the roof of the house, eating what the cook gave him, accepting a few dollars a week, which he tried to save. His constitution was in no shape to endure." In the end he becomes ill and is sent to Bellevue, that catch-all for the impoverished of New York City (today as well as in 1900).

"No more weakly looking object ever strolled out into the spring sunshine than the once hale, lusty manager. All his corpulency had fled. His face was thin and pale, his hands white, his body flabby. Clothes and all, he weighed but one hundred and thirty-five pounds. Some old garments had been given him-a cheap brown coat and misfit pair of trousers. Also some change and advice. He was told to apply to the charities." The rest of the story is the painful one of Hurstwood's attempts - sometimes successful - to beg, his ineffectually carried-out plan to confront Carrie at her stage door and ask for money, and at last his falling into the company of a curious, passionate individual - "ex-soldier turned religionist" - who was wont to stand at the corner of Twenty-sixth Street and Broadway, intersected by Fifth Avenue, every night. This man, cloaked in a great cape and known as the Captain, was known for his nightly confrontation of the theatre crowd, and any other crowd which passed that way, for the sole purpose of securing 15 cents - just 15 cents for each of his men who stood there in line, often for hours - for the night's lodging. The evangelical tone of the Captain's cajoling passers-by for money; the spectacle of those motley men who stood in line until handed their particular 15 cents and then stepped back to wait; the significant step taken by Hurstwood into that waiting line on a particular night; and the finale - the "march to bed," from 26th Street to an 8th Street lodging house: the entire **episode** is a masterpiece of vivid, poignant detail, perhaps the most memorable passage of pathos and **irony**, in its reflection of the grim private and public destinies involved, in the whole novel. The chapter is also Hurstwood's chapter, since it contains his last rational or semi-rational gestures to survive. Seated upon "the miserable bunk in the small, lightless chamber allotted to him," he tells himself, "I've got to eat, or I'll die."

CHAPTER 46. STIRRING TROUBLED WATERS

Drouet reappears here, not, as Carrie imagines, to castigate her for anything, but to renew contact in his old good-natured way. It is from him, too, that the final revelation about Hurstwood's theft from Fitzgerald and Moy's come to Carrie. To her credit, the revelation evokes in her not hatred but sympathy, with some imaginings that he took the money on her account. Her response is human: "Poor fellow! What a thing to have had hanging over his head all the time." Drouet, of course, although he fancies he is winning Carrie back as he dines with her, hasn't a chance of renewing his former relationship.

Carrie also encounters Hurstwood here, for what will turn out to be the last time; he had been hanging about the theatre for nights and nights to ask for help. Again, her response is human, and she is able to harbor no resentment toward him upon seeing his wretched condition. Yet she is also, strangely enough, in possession now of the fact of his former thievery, about which he deceived her as he deceived her about his marriage and their own marriage. She hands him what cash she is carrying, and disappears into the gloom.

Another indication that this chapter attempts to tie up loose ends of all the humanity caught up in the sage of Sister Carrie is her accidental meeting of Mr. Ames again, at the Vances'. Thus the reader is entitled to the altered response of a changed Carrie on this occasion: "She could hardly tell why the one-time keen interest in him was no longer with her. Unquestionably, it was because at that time he had represented something which she did not have; but this she did not understand. Success had given her the momentary feeling that she was now blessed with much of which he would approve." But again this young man has his effect upon her, making her feel "failure" by his observation that she should go into more serious drama, at the same time arousing her vanity by telling her she has the face and the disposition for it.

Comment

Dreiser is saying, through the remarks of Ames, something most significant and definitive to his own interpretation of the "meaning" of *Sister Carrie*. He shows Carrie as a tragic personage and gives the "whys" of her tragedy. He is also giving us, in a way, his statement on art, its meaning for him. Ames speaks to Carrie thus: "'Well,' he said, as one pleased with a puzzle, 'the expression in your face is one that comes out in different things. You get the same thing in a pathetic song or any picture that moves you deeply. It's a thing the world likes to see, because it's a natural expression of its longing.' Carrie gazed without exactly getting the import of what he meant. 'The world is always struggling to express itself,' he went on. "Most people are not capable of voicing their feelings. They depend upon others. That is what genius is for. One man expresses their desires for them in music; another one in poetry; another one in a play. Sometimes nature does it in a face-it makes the face representative of all desire. That's what has happened in your case.'" And so Carrie finally gets the idea that her look is something that represents the world's longing. It is Dreiser's view (or at least one view) of the meaning of art; it is also the interpretation, and the final representation, of Carrie herself; for that is how we will soon leave her, "representing the world's longing," including her own.

CHAPTER 47: THE WAY OF THE BEATEN: A HARP IN THE WIND

All the characters in the novel are brought into quick, final, ironic focus in this closing chapter. Foremost attention is given to Hurstwood and his increasing acquaintance with the charities of New York City of the 1900s. The author intends to document, almost as Michael Harrington has "documented" poverty in the America of the 1960s in The Other America, the realm of poverty-its avenues, outlets, and almost certain disasters. Hurstwood gets to know the Sisters of Mercy on Fifteenth Street, as well as Fleishmann, the baker who gives cut loaves of bread at midnight each evening to all who will come and get it. He also becomes accustomed to the endless, miserable waiting lines for these charitable offerings. "By January he had about concluded that the game was up with him. Life had always seemed a precious thing, but now constant want and weakened vitality had made the charms of earth rather dull and inconspicuous." These are the excruciating details of poverty, which have at last come to a focus in Hurstwood, whose state by now is somewhat illogical and incoherent. On his last "fifteen cent night," he reaches his cubicle and undresses, tucking his clothes under the door. He turns out the gas. "After a few minutes, in which he reviewed nothing, but merely hesitated, he turned the gas on again, but applied no match. Even then he stood there, hidden wholly in that kindness which is night, while the uprising fumes filled the room. When the odor reached his nostrils, he quit his attitude and fumbled for the bed. 'What's the use? he said, weakly, as he stretched himself to rest."

After arranging for a short glimpse of Charles Drouet going his old merry, unthinking way, as well as for a glance at Mrs. Hurstwood accompanying her beautiful, cold daughter with her newly acquired son-in-law on their way to sail for Europe, the author turns to his final treatment of the heroine: it is his closing statement. "Thus in life there is ever the intellectual and the emotional nature-the mind that reasons, and the mind that feels... . Man has not yet comprehended the dreamer any more than he has the ideal... . And it must be remembered that reason had little part in this Chicago dawning, she saw the city offering more of loveliness than she had ever known, and instinctively, by force of her moods alone, clung to it. In fine raiment and elegant surroundings, men seemed to be contented. Hence she drew near these things. Chicago, New York; Drouet, Hurstwood; the world of fashion and the world of stage-these were but incidents. Not them, but that which they represented, she longed for. Time proved the representation false." Against the "laws" and "conventions" Dreiser opposes the unsophisticated, emotional, instinctual nature of Carrie. "Not evil, but longing for that which is better more often directs the steps of the erring. Not evil, but goodness more often allures the feeling mind unused to reason."

Yet we leave Carrie sitting alone, "an illustration of the devious ways by which one who feels, rather than reasons, may be led in the pursuit of beauty."

Comment

Dreiser's closing lines, of course, are the reiteration of the philosophy of determinism which has governed the novel, just as the entire final chapter emphasizes once more the author's refusal to judge or moralize against his characters. "Oh, blind strivings of the human heart! Onward, onward, it saith, and where beauty leads it follows... . It is when the feet weary and hope seems vain that the heartaches and the longings arise. Know, then, that for you is neither surfeit nor content. In your rocking chair, by your window dreaming, shall you long, alone. In your rocking chair, by your window, shall you dream such happiness as you may never feel." We are left with Carrie rocking, rocking with the burden of her own and "the world's" impossible longings.

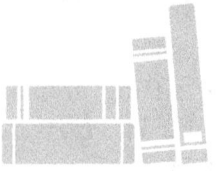

SISTER CARRIE

CHARACTER ANALYSES

SISTER CARRIE

Sister Carrie is, first of all, "sister" Carrie, a term which suggests both her ignorance and her innocence - and, most importantly, her instincts - as she confronts the metropolis and her destiny there. In the Carrie we see at the end of the novel, the ignorance and the innocence have, for the most part, been replaced by experience, some of it "awakening" experience. But it is instinct-chiefly represented by Dreiser as desire and as Carrie's emotional potential-that really governs her actions. Carrie is essentially nonaggressive and passive. She has often been contrasted to Isabel Archer, one of Henry Jame's major heroines, in *Portrait of a Lady*, who is an aggressive young American girl and is said to "affront" her destiny-that is, to go out and actively seek it. Nor is Carrie capable of being mean or vicious: on the occasion of her ultimate desertion of the sinking Hurstwood, she reflects on what both he and Drouet had done for her, feeling guilty because she hates to treat badly anyone who has been good to her.

But the one thing that will move Sister Carrie in behalf of her own interests-from the first few days in the Hanson flat, even-is her strong desire for pleasure. According to the materialistic formula which governs every one of Dreiser's characters in the book (except Mr. Ames), pleasure comes from money, and is very often symbolized by clothes. Carrie's first gesture toward her destiny-the acceptance of twenty dollars from Drouet-is motivated by her desire to escape from the drudgery and drabness of the Hansons' life, to look as pretty as the girls she passes on Chicago's streets-in short, to move "up." Dreiser asserts that, after all, her impoverished background has, naturally enough, supplied her with only "an average little conscience," and in accepting Drouet's early overtures she is very little influenced by "home principles." She is a "half-equipped little knight"; yet the reader is led to believe from the first that Carrie contains more potential than the two men she is linked within the novel. The author refers to this sometimes as "spirit," sometimes as "imagination," sometimes as "emotional greatness." (Dreiser suggests the latter in saying of Hurstwood that "he did not understand the nature of emotional greatness. He had never learned that a person might be emotionally-instead of intellectually-great." Whether or not Carrie is emotionally "great" - and it is difficult for the reader to see her, in her drifting passivity, as quite that-it is nevertheless this instinctual quality of expressing emotions that makes her first chance theatrical venture a success, and leads her into later, legitimate theatrical acclaim.

We are thus led to conclude that there is unconscious emotional greatness in Carrie, which importantly expresses, as Dreiser tells us through Mr. Ames, the universal longings of mankind. Ames tells her, in an attempt to get her to better assess her potential and use it, that the "world is always struggling to express itself, ... Most people are not capable of voicing their feelings. They depend upon others... . Sometimes nature does it in a face-it makes the face representative of all desire. That's what has happened in your case." Yet it remains ironic that Carrie is to express through her face the pathos of the world's yearnings, since she is but vaguely aware of it, to the end. Here too, in giving her such a face and in giving her that later opportunity in New York to become an actress, chance, whether of nature or of environment, has played the largest part. For when Carrie, upon her first meeting with Mr. Ames, feels the pain of not understanding something, it is but a preview of her final state, when, rocking and dreaming, we leave her as the "representation" of the world's discontent-the world which can feel, can pursue, but cannot reason, chiefly because circumstances have kept it below the level of the reasoning mind.

DROUET

Drouet, a representative of a class which was arising in this period because of the giant expansion of industry, is a "drummer" or, to us, a traveling salesman. Along with this he is a "masher," "one whose dress or manners are calculated to elicit the admiration of susceptible young women." We see Drouet as somewhat vain and superficial (and it is this very egotism which prevents him from being sensitive enough to the changing Carrie, for he believes that her early brooding and depression spring from her loneliness for him, as she awaits his return from traveling. But we also sympathize with him as a good-hearted, spontaneous person, "caught" also in the circumstances which placed material gain and pleasure above all else in the American society of the 1900s. Drouet is as nonreflective as Carrie (or more so) and less calculating than Hurstwood. But he is ready, as we recall, with a genuine offer of help to Carrie (for it is instinct and circumstances that inevitably draw them into alliance later) or with a dime for a bum on the streets. He is not a tragic figure, but there is pathos for the reader in the very image of him, later in the novel, as merrily proceeding on the same vain assumptions which governed him at the beginning. When Drouet meets Carrie again, he himself has not changed; and our last glimpse of him, after Carrie, who has changed and rejects his gestures of old affection toward her, is one of his usual pursuits of pleasure-putting on a good appearance and going after some fine-stepping girls.

HURSTWOOD

Hurstwood, although at the top social level of which Dreiser writes, is just as much a wisp in the wind of circumstance and environment as are the other characters-perhaps, in his case, because he and his family feel the pull and push toward the really, luxuriously rich. Again, material ambition drives the individual, and chance controls his destiny. Hurstwood, when we first meet him in Chicago, is very much a part of his milieu of physical comfort, solid respectability, professional success, and social interchange with the great and near-great. We understand that his life at Fitzgerald and Moy's is his real life, whereas his existence with his family is the facade, but a facade to be sensibly preserved. The early Hurstwood is secure, shrewd and cautious. But when chance begins to take over his fate, the downward slope begins (although he himself is but dimly aware of this, even in New York, until the very end and his suicide). Faced with his cold and selfish wife, her disinterest, and their grasping children, he meets Carrie and falls into the "tragedy of affection" - especially the tragedy of affection rekindled in middle age. From this meeting and the growing relationship he moves to the very center (and peak) of his existence in the novel-that is, to the sheerest accident of his theft from his employers, so irrevocable to his future destiny. Dreiser's lengthy description of the insecurity and indecision of this scene emphasizes how truly there was no previous intention of thievery on Hurstwood's part and how large a part chance plays. He found the safe unlocked, his own thoughts were fuzzy from liquor to which he was unaccustomed, and he felt himself at that moment quite trapped by the imperative demands for money from his obsessed wife. Although Hurstwood's desire for escape from his current dilemma is real enough, his act of stealing is an accident. Yet from this central act stems his ultimate downfall. Thus it is through Hurstwood most of all that Dreiser proves his point about the amassed force of a materialistic society against the faltering, unaware individual who is ill-equipped by nature or by environment to reason or to reflect upon his state and upon the consequences of his actions. Deprived of his comfortable, secure milieu when he comes to New York, it is a short step to the apathy which forces Hurstwood gradually down to the Bowery and his death.

MRS. HURSTWOOD

Mrs. Hurstwood, as Dreiser tells us, "was the type of the woman who has ever endeavored to shine and has been more or less chagrined at the evidences of superior capability in this direction elsewhere. Her knowledge of life extended to that little conventional round of society of which she was not - but longed to be - a member. She was not without realization already that this thing was impossible, so far as she was concerned. For her daughter, she hoped better things." These remarks truly suggest what we perceive of this woman's character. Whatever attracted Hurstwood to her at the beginning (and we are told that there was some small affection between them, some basis for a union) has died away, and we see them living essentially separate lives, where tolerance prevails so long as the "dried tinder" of separate frustrations and irritations is not kindled. Hurstwood, the conscientious provider while his two children have been growing up, is vaguely aware of his wife's capacity for vanity, and even for hatred, if obstacles should be placed in the path of her-or her children's-climb upward. Thus as Mrs. Hurstwood feels increasingly neglected socially by her husband, her sense of fatal affront to her vanity increases, and at length brings about the explosion and split in their relationship. She then perceives that she can more effectively realize her social aims without her husband, provided she retains his material wealth. At the novel's end we see that she has indeed calculated "something better" for her daughter, who has married well and is off to Europe.

JESSICA AND GEORGE HURSTWOOD

Jessica And George Hurstwood are to be regarded as the inevitable generation (generation of vipers, perhaps) which would spring from the union of two such materialists as their parents. Theirs has not been the "lovely home atmosphere" which Dreiser insists is necessary to "make strong and just the natures cradled and nourished within it." These two young people reach some sort of adulthood as self-centered, indifferent, unloving creatures, completely motivated by what money can get for them. They are the generation (such as the son of Samuel Griffiths in *An American Tragedy*) that will cling tenaciously to its "ingroupism" and will ruthlessly exclude all outsiders.

THE HANSONS

The Hansons are, of course, at the lower levels in their climb upward. Carrie's brother-in-law's way "up" is obviously to "save." "He was of a clean, saving disposition, and had already paid a number of monthly installments on two lots far out on the West Side. His ambition was someday to build a house on them." But Hanson's way, necessarily, will be one of drudgery, plodding, self-denial-that "dull round of days" without pleasure or even much thought of pleasure. And Carrie perceives early in her short stay with them that her sister, Minnie, has taken on her husband's view of life, too. "She was not a thin, though rugged woman of twenty-seven, with ideas of life colored by her husband's, and fast hardening into narrower conceptions of pleasure and duty than had ever been hers in a thoroughly circumscribed youth." The Hansons set their sights much lower than the Hurstwoods but their motivations are exactly the same: to increase their material well-being.

MISS OSBORNE

Miss Osborne, Carrie's theatrical friend, would have made a suitable match for Drouet, perhaps, since their mothlike characters seem similar. She is the girl who takes life easily, always seeking a little better for herself. But she is unreflecting, without the depressions that beset Carrie. She is not at all destined to be great in the theatre; and she good-naturedly praises, encourages, and really likes her young friend. She, like Drouet, will be able to go merrily on her way throughout life undisturbed by intimations of intellect, reason, or soul.

THE VANCES

The Vances similarly represent another "level" of the American society Dreiser is intent upon describing in detail. Their class is below that of the Hurstwoods, yet they manage to live well.

Indeed, throughout the novel, they are always seen in the pursuit of pleasure, whether of appearance, gastronomy, or "art." It is no doubt deliberately withheld from the reader what the actual source of their income is: they represent that class which would mushroom into the succeeding decades as one which probably "lives beyond its means" but, with luck, eludes bankruptcy.

MR. AMES

Mr. Ames is the indubitable intellectual in the novel and insofar as he is developed as an intellectual he is "outside" the propelling forces of materialism in the novel. Apparently Dreiser was (in this, his first novel) working out through Ames his own ideas on art and beauty. Hence we have his remarks (significant to Carrie) on an item of beauty-a pin-worn by a woman on the occasion of the gastronomical display at Sherry's. And we have his suggestion (again disturbing to Carrie) that there could be "bad" books as well as "good" books. Later, he will suggest again the idea of "choice" to Carrie, in describing to her what her artistic potential is. At the same time, in persuading Carrie that she has a face in which people can perceive their own yearnings and discontent, he is also speaking for Dreiser on art: art itself plays back to the people their universal longings.

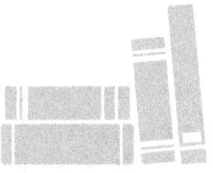

SISTER CARRIE

CRITICAL COMMENTARY

Since in the foregoing pages there has been an implication of divided critical opinion on the literary worth of Theodore Dreiser, it may be well to note at this point that his critics do indeed separate into two rather distinct schools of thought, one as adversely critical as the other is enthusiastically complimentary (with the customary shades of compromise in the views in between). The adversely critical school, its pronouncements dating of course from the first appearances of his work around the turn of the century, ranges from opposition to his "barbaric naturalism" in conflict with a "genteel tradition" in literature to more recent objections to his writing on aesthetic or ideational grounds. The school of enthusiastic approval is one inclined to abide by his "new **realism**" and to applaud his vehement "socio-political" views expressed through fiction.

Two chief objectors to Dreiser's work may be taken as representative - one contemporary to him, the other contemporary to us. The notion of Dreiser's "barbaric naturalism" is set forth by Stuart P. Sherman in "The Barbaric Naturalism of Mr. Dreiser" (first appearing in *The Nation*, December 2, 1915; later published in *On Contemporary Literature*, New York, 1917) who begins by remarking ironically that "the present age is fearless and is freeing itself from illusions. Now, for the first time in history, men are facing unabashed the facts of life. 'Death or life,' we cry, 'give us only reality!' Now, for the first time in the history of English literature, fiction is become a flawless mirror held up to the living world." Of Dreiser's first five works (*Sister Carrie, Jennie Gerhardt, The Financier, The Titan* and *The Genius*) Sherman claims, "I do not find any moral value in them, nor any memorable beauty - of their truth I shall speak later; but I am greatly impressed by them as serious representatives of a new note in American literature, coming from that 'ethnic' element of our mixed population which, as we are assured by competent authorities, is to redeem us from Puritanism and insure our artistic salvation. They abundantly illustrate, furthermore, the methods and intentions of our recent courageous, veracious **realism**. Before we thank God for it let us consider a little more closely what is offered us." In an effort to detail (or possibly to destroy) Dreiser's work, Sherman suggests that the "real distinction between one generation and another is in the thing which each takes for its master truth - in the thing which each recognizes as the essential reality for it." Yet Sherman insists that, contrary to Dreiser's "naturalistic method" (praised, as we shall see, by his complimentary critics), "there is no such thing as a 'cross-section' or 'slice' or 'photograph' of life in art-least of all in the realistic novel. The use of these catchwords is but a clever hypnotizing pass of the artist, employed to win the assent of the reader to the reality of the show, and, in some cases, to evade moral responsibility for any questionable features of the exhibition. A realistic novel no more than any other kind of a novel can escape a being composition involving preconception, imagination, and divination." (It is, incidentally, on this very issue that H. G. Wells found cause to praise *An American Tragedy*, Dreiser's first immediately popular success, asserting that "far more than life-size rendering of a poor little representative corner of American existence, lighted up by a flash of miserable tragedy," the novel tells a "large, harsh superficial truth" about American society of the 1920s. To Wells, then, as to other critics approving Dreiser's thesis the "essential reality" or "master truth" of his generation is this illumination of his society, that society itself.)

But Sherman (as does Lionel Trilling in a later essay) is inclined to question the "adequacy" of Dreiser's ideas, suggesting that "in the case of any specified novelist, the facts chosen and the pattern assumed by them are determined by his central theory or 'philosophy of life'; and this is precisely criticism's justification for inquiring into the adequacy of any novelist's general ideas." Thus Sherman finds Dreiser's first five novels "bewildering masses of detail," whose "impressive unity of effect ... is due to the fact that they are all illustrations of a crude and naively simple naturalistic philosophy.... The central truth about man is that he is an animal amenable to no law but the law of his own temperament, doing as he desires, subject only to the limitations of his power.

The male of the species is characterized by cupidity, pugnacity, and a simian inclination for the other sex. The female is a soft, vain pleasure-seeking creature, devoted to personal adornment, and quite helplessly susceptible to the flattery of the male. In the struggles which arise in the jungle through the conflicting appetites of its denizens the victory goes to the animal most physically fit and mentally ruthless, unless the weaklings, resisting absorption, combine against him and crush him by sheer force of numbers. The idea that civilization is a sham Mr. Dreiser sometimes sets forth explicitly and sometimes he conveys it by a process known among journalists as 'coloring the news.' When Sister Carrie yields to the seductive drummer, Drouet, Mr. Dreiser judicially weighs the advantages and disadvantages attendant on the condition of being a well-kept mistress." And this critic has a good deal more to say on Dreiser's emphasis on man's animality, on Dreiser's supposed debunking of "righteousness," "conventions," "routine," "respectability." It is Sherman's conclusion, then, that by "thus eliminating distinctively human motives and making animal instincts the supreme factors in human life, Mr. Dreiser reduces the problem of the novelist to the lowest possible terms ... he has chosen only to illustrate the unrestricted flow of temperament." Thus he concludes also that Dreiser's novels are loaded with irrelevant detail, and do not come up to the standard for a "realistic novel," which is a "representation based upon a theory of human conduct." Choosing to ignore the possibility of "society" as an evil (which is what those who praise Dreiser claim), Sherman concentrates on the "jungle-motive" in his writing: "if you expect to gain credence for the notion that your hero can have any woman in Chicago or New York that he puts his paw upon, you had probably better lead up to it by a detailed account of the street-railway system in those cities. It will necessitate the loading of your pages with a tremendous baggage of irrelevant detail. It will not sound much like art, ... But it will produce an overwhelming impression of reality, which the reader will carry with him into the next chapter where you are laying bare the 'chemistry' of the human animal."

A more recent essay by Lionel Trilling (*The Liberal Imagination*, New York, 1945) which first expounds on the influence of V. L. Parrington (*Main Currents in American Thought*; *Literary History of the United States*), as a "liberal" supporter of literary **realism**, on American critical thought, secondarily turns to Parrington's somewhat representative favorable evaluation of Dreiser. The essay is essentially an argument, however, against what Trilling sees as a too prevalent tendency to divorce "**realism**" from "ideas," or "aesthetics." And he suggests that "this belief in the incompatibility of mind and reality is exemplified by the doctrinaire indulgence which liberal intellectuals have always displayed toward Theodore Dreiser, an indulgence which becomes the worthier of remark when it is contrasted with the liberal severity toward Henry James [the other part of Mr. Trilling's point is that James is too genteel, too aesthetic an author for such critics]. Dreiser and James: with that juxtaposition we are immediately at the dark and bloody crossroads where literature and politics meet." This "liberal criticism," as Trilling would have it, sees Dreiser's literary faults as "social and political virtues. It was Parrington who established the formula for the liberal criticism of Dreiser by calling him a 'peasant': when Dreiser thinks stupidly, it is because he has the slow stubbornness of a peasant; when he writes badly, it is because he is impatient of the sterile literary gentility of the bourgeoisie. It is as if wit, and flexibility of mind, and perception, and knowledge were to be equated with aristocracy and political reaction, while dullness and stupidity must naturally suggest a virtuous democracy... ." Trilling views this position of praising Dreiser essentially for his social message as a rather false, and a rather American, idea of literary **realism**: we approve Dreiser's books because they "have the awkwardness, the chaos, the heaviness which we associate with 'reality.' In the American metaphysics, reality is always material reality, hard, resistant, unformed, impenetrable and unpleasant. And that mind is alone felt to be trustworthy which most resembles this reality by most nearly reproducing the sensations it affords."

By proceeding with the contrast between Dreiser and James, Trilling is able to illuminate further this disparity between their critics: "The 'odors of the shop' are real, and to those who breathe them they guarantee a sense of vitality from which James is debarred. The idea of intellectual honor is not real, and to that chimera James was devoted." And, by the same token,

"Dreiser is to be accepted and forgiven because his faults are the sad, lovable, honorable faults of reality itself, or of America itself - huge, inchoate, struggling toward expression, caught between the dream of raw power and the dream of morality." (Trilling also points out, incidentally, that one of Dreiser's faults of style would seem to be a lack of that very colloquialism for which he is sometimes acclaimed - Middle West **diction**, for instance - "if we are to talk of bookishness, it is Dreiser who is bookish; he is precisely literary in the bad sense; he is full of flowers of rhetoric and shines with paste gems; at hundreds of points his **diction** is not only genteel but fancy.")

What Lionel Trilling is chiefly concerned about with Dreiser's liberal critics, though, is that they too indiscriminately accepted, indulged what were rather generalized even naive ideas couched in sometimes rough and repetitious prose; Dreiser as philosopher, Trilling asserts, "is likely to be not only foolish but vulgar. He thinks as the modern crowd thinks when it decides to think; religion and morality are nonsense, 'religionists' and moralists are fakes, tradition is a fraud, what is man but matter and impulses, mysterious 'chemisms,' what value has life anyway?" Trilling will certainly grant Dreiser's earnestness that he meant his ideas; but this did not guarantee his philosophical or aesthetic success, and his liberal critics have too readily and uncritically accepted him. "This is the liberal criticism, in the direct line of Parrington, which establishes the social responsibility of the writer and then goes on to say that, apart from his duty of resembling reality as much as possible, he is not really responsible for anything, not even for his ideas. The scope of reality being what it is, ideas are held to be mere 'details,' and, what is more, to be details which, if attended to, have the effect of diminishing reality." The liberal criticism, according to Trilling, urges us "to deal impatiently with ideas." It is possible that Theodore Dreiser would not have disagreed much with the foregoing adverse criticism of his work, recalling one of his remarks to his friend H. L. Mencken (in a letter previously quoted): "You see, Mencken, unlike yourself I am biased. I was born poor." His basic premise (and it seems to survive the accusations of "Darwinism," "jungle-motive," "animal-like" characters) was that society of his time was evil; or, as Sister Carrie in her muddled reflections figured it out, "there was something cruel somewhere." Another of his admirers, James Farrell, puts it this way - "evil is social.... He has related social causation to the individual pattern of destiny." To Farrell (and countless other critics down to the present: Randolph Bourne, F. Scott Fitzgerald, Sherwood Anderson, Alfred Kazin, F. O. Matthiessen), Dreiser's social determinism represented a "healthy pessimism," especially healthy for his own time. And his characters, far from being so subjectively animalistic, have a universal quality, according to Randolph Bourne, for whom Carrie or Clyde symbolize "that desire within us that pounds in manifold guise against the iron walls of experiences." As F. O. Matthiessen explains (what Dreiser himself set forth in an essay titled "The Essential Tragedy of Life"), this essential tragedy of life is "in man's consciousness of the immense force beyond his control, and of the basic fact that he does not use these forces, but is used by them." In Dreiser's own words, "As I see him, man is much more led or pushed than he is leading or pushing." Matthiessen further sums it up by saying, "Rejecting the nineteenth-century myth of the free individual, which his experience has proved to him to be false, he has now gone to the opposite pole in portraying an individual without any purposive will."

The most enthusiastic proponents of Dreiser's books would probably, in point of fact, place his detractors (represented above by Stuart Sherman and Lionel Trilling) among the "Puritans" complaining of an "anti-Puritan" in their midst. This is the gist of Sherwood Anderson's previously mentioned praise, for example, in dedicating *Horses and Men* to Dreiser and in acknowledging the debt younger writers owed to Dreiser: "The prose writers in America who follow Dreiser will have much to do that he has never done ... but, because of him, those who follow will never have to face the road through the wilderness of Puritan denial, the road that Dreiser faced alone." A similar position is taken by Alfred Kazin (*On Native Grounds*, New York, 1942), who sees Dreiser as "trampling down the lies of gentility and Victorianism, of Puritanism and academicism. Dreiser was the primitive, the man from the abyss, the stranger who had grown up outside the middle-class Protestant morality and so had no need to accept its sanctions." Alfred Kazin's words may be allowed to stand as the final ones on this dilemma between the two schools of Dreiserian criticism. He reminds us, "who can forget the image of the rocking chair in *Sister Carrie*, where from this cradle endlessly rocking man stares forever at a world he is not too weak but too bemused to change? And it is this lack of smartness ... that explains why we do not know what to do with Dreiser today." Dreiser in fact looked upon himself as an anomalous, mixed creature, writing in *A Traveler at Forty* that "there is in me the spirit of a lonely child" that "cries when it is frightened; and then there is a coarse, vulgar exterior which fronts the world defiantly and bids all and sundry go to the devil." "Fearless, grim, compassionate and hateful," his friend Edgar Lee Masters described him poetically. We might recall for a moment two of Dreiser's most effective passages - Dreiser at his best - in two different novels: the final chapter of *Sister Carrie*, wherein all the characters parade past for a concluding look; or the epilogue of *An American Tragedy*, where those who at the beginning held tight to their illusions and refused to face facts are now repeating the same cycle, in seeming obliviousness to the monstrous, tragic changes which have been wrought in lives around them (such as the death of the **protagonist** Clyde

Griffiths), unaware that grim fates are about to be acted out all over again. As Matthiessen suggests (of *Sister Carrie*), "by picking up and dropping again the threads of these other lives in his final pages, Dreiser enforces our sensation of isolation, of a world divested of lasting human contacts." And, as a matter of fact, this same mood is conveyed in Clyde Griffiths' final two days before his execution. These poignant passages: the final-days reflections of Clyde along with the epilogue - his futility about the world's future understanding of him; the farewell image of Carrie in her rocking chair, dreaming of happiness that she "may never feel" verify most forcibly Dreiser's unceasing skepticism about the hard, real world. At the same time, they convey a humanist's compassionate understanding of man's striving imagination, and possibly (but a quality his adverse critics would by no means grant) the author's hope, a little wistful, for something eventually transcendent in man through the greater development of his reason over his instinct and, subsequently, the growth of a sense of responsibility for fellow men in his society.

SISTER CARRIE

THE ACCOMPLISHMENTS OF THEODORE DREISER

THE AMERICAN DREAM EXPOSED

From the moment Theodore Dreiser's *Sister Carrie* was presented to the public (and the press) in 1900, notwithstanding the inner sanctum controversy at Doubleday and the suppression of the novel to a minimum number of copies casually issued without the customary advertising (and it should be noted here that this suppression by the publisher has since become somewhat of a myth, no little of the credit for the perpetuation of which can be attributed to the author's friend, correspondent and critic, H. L. Mencken), it was clear that in many ways the novel represented the first little nuclear explosion in what would eventually amount to full-scale atomic war waged by Dreiser upon "the American Dream." (It is a battle which has of course continued into contemporary literature.) Not that Dreiser's manner was very explosive; on the contrary, it was his matter-of-fact, nonjudgmental denuding of that myth of the American Dream - the illusion that every poor boy has a chance of becoming President or of marrying Cinderella - rich and living happily ever after - which outraged, startled, perhaps frightened the first readers and some of the critics. Carrie Meeber, Dreiser's little "half-equipped soldier," as he called her, quietly shattered - with an almost maddening passiveness and lack of awareness - too much of the moral, socio-economic, and philosophical American tradition. The wealth and fame with any pleasure at her fingertips, which Carrie has attained at the end of Dreiser's novel, come to her through several very familiar channels traditionally regarded as encouraging young girls to sin and ruination. She is a country girl who moves to the city to seek her future. The success she gradually begins to find comes to her through the stage, always a scene of dubious repute to the lingering New England conscience. Worst of all, her real start in life, and her later sustenance, are provided by the liaisons she enters into with Drouet and Hurstwood. Yet the contradiction which Carrie represented at the novel's conclusion - the unresolved inner conflict and lack of self-awareness must have become a contradiction hardly bearable in her readers' hearts, too. Carrie is never punished for her apparent flouting of the **conventions** of morality. There is little sign that her creator regarded her actions as sinful; they were merely inevitable, given her circumstances. At the same time, Carrie is not happy or content with her success and material well-being when we leave her rocking, with quiet bewilderment and an inexplicable sense of isolation, at the window of her luxury apartment. It is possible that Carrie's second sin - that of not finding happiness in material success - was the one which at heart disturbed her readers most, for it upset the American equation of money with contentment.

THE INDIVIDUAL AGAINST UNIVERSAL FORCES: DETERMINISM

Essentially, Dreiser's **themes** are few and are continually reiterated, just as his attitudes and intentions - while not always cohesive and unified - are relatively clear. He looked upon the individual of his time (and, we infer from the whole panorama of his work, human beings universally) as caught up in both internal and external struggles which were yet interrelated. His young protagonists, so often born poor, are driven both by natural instinct (with which weak reason struggles ineffectively in them) and by the glittering external circumstance of American affluence, to seek out their desires - pleasure, a good appearance (clothes are always status symbols in his writings), luxurious living arrangements and glamorous professions. For example, the single urge which can rouse Carrie from her basic timidity (when she has first arrived in Chicago and is installed in her brother-in-law's flat) is her desire for pleasure, in this instance the wish to attend the theatre, for which she nags her sister to solicit Hanson's permission. Similarly, Carrie's first step outside the path of conventional propriety - accepting money from Drouet - is motivated by her yearning to look as pretty as the smartly dressed young women she sees on the Chicago streets. Likewise, Carrie's transition, from Drouet's cozy living arrangements in Chicago, to the more and more disagreeably downgraded life she lives with Hurstwood in New York, to the residence she ultimately takes up in fancy metropolitan hotels, is movement upward toward comfort and luxury, brought about of course by her success in a glamorous, flashy profession, the theatre.

Yet Carrie is not only an individual - and an autobiographical throwback to Dreiser's sisters - but she is also a universal character, as universally human in her strivings as a Clyde Griffiths (*An American Tragedy*) or a Hurstwood. Randolph Bourne, reviewing Dreiser's *The "Genius"*, comments on this universality in Dreiser, his ability to get beneath the "conventional super-structure" of the contemporary novel of his time, as being a great virtue. He remarks that Dreiser's heroes are not really "*Sister Carrie* or *the Titan* or *the Genius*, but that desire within us that pounds in manifold guise against the iron walls of experience." Dreiser's conviction of this indubitable pressure of nature and environmental circumstance has been termed "mechanism" or "determinism." A close friend of the author's once referred to this seeming universal force as "the mass and weight of the stupendous life-tide," a force which sweeps away all his individuals, so that "not they, but It, must be regarded as the hero of the tale." (This may be a satisfactory philosophic view of it although in the following paragraphs we may be able to specify the "It" more concretely as "society.") In any case, such a life-view rather naturally nominates an author for the ranks of the skeptics, since there seem to be so few alternatives or real choices available to his characters.

DREISER'S HUMANE, SYMPATHETIC ATTITUDE: HUMANISM

As F. O. Matthiessen points out, however, and as all Dreiser's writings demonstrate, "He never really adhered to the pitiless implications of the Darwinian universe. As he admired the strong and sympathized with the weak, he became deeply involved with them both." This dual involvement reflects his own mixed personality and family background, his relationships with the father whom he viewed as ineffectual against life, the mother whom he regarded as tender and strong, and the brothers and sisters so trapped in the mesh of circumstances. Thus it is in that same nonmoralizing, matter-of-fact treatment of his characters and their actions in a bewildering universe that we are obliged to note that Dreiser's skepticism is mingled with compassion: he is a humanist too. Perhaps he is a humanist propelled, as James Farrell has suggested, by a "healthy pessimism." He simply insists on seeing the facts of life as they really are, and as they change over a period of time. Carrie, for example, on the eve of her desertion of the down-and-out Hurstwood feels genuine appreciation for what both the men in her life have done for her, and sincere regret at being forced to act in a way which may hurt Hurstwood. Nevertheless, Carrie is forced to go in her own behalf, given the apathy and now-proven failure of Hurstwood in the face of the alien, hostile world he has found in New York City. Carrie is Dreiser's pragmatist, molding and changing herself with the signs and the times, responding to an altered environment in terms of her own needs. But Hurstwood's life too is pervaded by the author's "healthy pessimism." Early in the novel the reader is briefed in cool detail on Hurstwood's background, on Hurstwood as a most perfect product of his environment and its standards - his solid respectability of home, family and profession combined with a cold, detached relationship with the members of his family, each selfishly after his own interests and ambitious to be moving up in the world. Dreiser describes Hurstwood's job as manager of Fitzgerald and Moy's, around which his existence really centers, because it offers him what makes him feel most alive and comfortable and secure: a chance to dress tastefully and expensively, an opportunity to mingle with some authority among the great and near-great, a situation which utilizes his most valuable, most cultivated qualities of shrewdness, cool efficiency and charm. Such details of Hurstwood's life, with their underlying implication of emptiness and lack of warmth, suggest strongly that when the props are knocked out from under him - as they are from the moment of Mrs. Hurstwood's rebellion which turns into a vicious suit for divorce and from the moment of his impulsive, inept thievery from his employers - his potential is for frustration, futility, apathy, and at last, despair. Thus in Hurstwood too Dreiser has managed to predict his failing struggle against bewildering adverse circumstances from the first day he declines to go job-hunting and sinks into the "Lethean waters" of reading and rocking in the womblike warmth of the flat, through to his suicide on the Bowery. At the same time the author has also predicted, both skeptically and humanistically, the inexplicability of Carrie's reaching the top, materialistically speaking, only to find herself bereft of real contentment, left at the end to rock and wonder about her own humanity.

DREISER'S OWN LIFE AS BACKGROUND MATERIAL

Dreiser's skepticism as well as his humanism ought to be regarded as "native" to him, the result of his own impoverished and unsatisfying youth, and verified by later experience and observation (in his first city employment, for example, or, later, as a reporter). His nonmoralizing nonjudgmental treatment of his material was just as inevitable, given these early intimate glances at the real facts of life. Sister Carrie's story, for example, is rather closely related to incidents in the life of one of his sisters who, having been supported by an architect in Chicago, found herself drawn toward the manager of Hannah and Hogg's, a famous restaurant/ bar. Like Carrie, she eloped with him to Canada, after he had stolen $15,000 from his employers (money later to be regretfully returned by the man, as Hurstwood does in the novel), and without her being aware of his married state. Dreiser's sister, again like Carrie, later found herself in financial straits in her life with the ex-manager, although the details of their life in actuality are a bit more sordid than those of Carrie's case with Hurstwood in the novel. Similarly, Carrie's delight and awe in discovering the metropolis may be paralleled with Dreiser's own excitement upon leaving home at fifteen for Chicago (as he has described it in his autobiographical writings).

It must be pointed out, however, that what Dreiser took from his own background into his writings - especially his attitudes, which are expressed as **themes** - was gradually solidified by the developing artist in him as principle or a kind of philosophy. As one of his biographers, Dorothy Dudley, points out, "Dreiser was one of those born outside the **convention**, and living outside of it." Just as some of his near-contemporaries, such as Edith Wharton and Henry James, wrote of the "genteel tradition" from within it because they happened to have been born in it, so Dreiser had to write outside of the **conventions** he had been excluded from. But this is perhaps why early reviewers of his writings may have felt so alienated by his works. As H. L. Mencken pointed out (in *A Book of Prefaces*, although he has expressed himself on Dreiser many times over a period of years), "Fully nine-tenths of the reviews of Dreiser's *The Titan* ... were devoted chiefly to indignant denunciations of the morals of Frank Cowperwood its central character... . They were Puritans writing for Puritans, and all they could see in Cowperwood was an anti-Puritan, and in his creator another." It is this very matter of Puritanism and anti-Puritanism for which Sherwood Anderson praised Dreiser in dedicating *Horses and Men* to him, saying that he represented "something gray and bleak and hurtful, that has been in the world perhaps forever," and assessing the debt that writers such as himself, John dos Passos and F. Scott Fitzgerald owed to Dreiser: "The prose writers in America who follow Dreiser will have much to do that he has never done ... but, because of him, those who follow will never have to face the road through the wilderness of Puritan denial, the road that Dreiser faced alone."

DREISER'S BLAST AT THE MATERIALISM OF AMERICA IN THE 1900S

It was of course the materialistic monomania of his own society and times which Dreiser viewed "from the outside." ("Outside" in the sense that he had been born and brought up outside of it, and also in the sense that he had, like the Sister Carries and the

Clyde Griffiths, wanted very naturally to get on the "inside" - the **theme** of the "outsider," in fact, figures largely in much of his writing.) Dreiser looked upon American society of the 1900s as so unstably concentrated upon money values that it was not surprising for it to produce insecure, indecisive people. Most of Carrie's "actions," we recall, in reality result from passivity and inaction, from her merely drifting into a new situation. F. O. Matthiessen aptly remarks that Dreiser's is a society "in which there are no real equals, and no equilibrium, but only people moving up and down." On that dollar-strewn "stairway to paradise," Dreiser's strong ones "get there at any price." Their motions upward are compulsive, their awareness of the "price" is kept at a minimum, and their ultimate disregard of fellow men in favor of their own survival is inevitable. Even Carrie, one of Dreiser's most sensitive characters, is little inclined to look back upon the past and its people with much regret as she steps up higher and higher. Likewise (in the words of another eminently qualified commentator of what it feels like to be "down" instead of "up" - Billie Holiday), in Dreiser's stories the strong gets more, while the weak ones fade: empty pockets don't ever make the grade." (*God Bless the Child that's Got His Own.*) For example, take Carrie in her confused reflections and her conflicts about what was right and what was wrong in her past and present with Drouet and Hurstwood. Trying to figure it all out to some conclusion which will help govern her subsequent actions, all she can come up with is "there was something cruel somewhere... ." According to Dreiser, what is cruel is the climbing society, on its way up without looking back or lending a helping hand to those below, in fact often trodding down the lower level. To him, this was a dangerous myth which he did his best to explode, quietly, into its hypocritical fragments proceeding in his typically deliberate way: "Trampling down," as Alfred Kazin phrases it, the lies of gentility and Victorianism, of Puritanism and academicism. Dreiser was the primitive, the man from the abyss, the stranger who had grown up outside the middle-class Protestant morality [of the Midwest] and so had no need to accept its sanctions." And his account of poverty was one of the first significant ones in American fiction.

THE WRITER AS MAN AND PHILOSOPHER

Perhaps Dreiser did seek all his life, as Farrell suggests, for a "theory of existence," hopefully for something in man which would "transcend" what he pragmatically observed was a far-too-frequent helplessness. Hence his skepticism is mixed with a humanism. It would appear, in fact, that Theodore Dreiser had something in common with a number of his characters: Carrie, Clyde Griffiths, Drouet, and Hurstwood. His biographer, Dorothy Dudley, could look upon him as a mixture of at least three types. She suggests that there was in Dreiser a Hurstwood/Samuel Griffiths competitive quality. (Samuel Griffiths is a successful manufacturer, uncle of Clyde Griffiths, in An American Tragedy.) There was as well (part of the time) the good-humored, companionable, even "masher" element of Drouet. Combined with these aspects was the creative person who could be anti-social and withdrawn. However, there is a useful bit of incisive self-characterization to be found in one of Dreiser's letters to H. L. Mencken in 1943 (two years before his death): "You see, Mencken, unlike yourself I am biased. I was born poor. For a time, in November and December, once, I went without shoes. I saw my beloved mother suffer from want - even worry and wring her hands in misery. And for that reason, perhaps - let it be what it will - I, regardless of whom or what, am for a social system that can and will do better than that for its members - those who try, however humbly - and more, wish to learn how to help themselves, but are nonetheless defeated by the trickeries" of those "who believe that money ... distinguishes them above all others." We need not, from these comments, make Dreiser out to have been an effective politician or reformer, or a very thorough, logical philosopher, or even a consistent, detached social critic. Yet such remarks on his part do seem to reinforce the attitudes and principles which emerge from his work. Born poor, he could never have been a Booth Tarkington type (writing comfortably of local Hoosier color, out of a nostalgia for the past and a sentimentalization of the present). As F. O. Matthiessen rather wryly explains it, "What prevented Dreiser from being seduced by the wistful charm that he knew to be the standard literary product of his native state [the 'folksy' writings of his Indiana colleague referred to above; or indeed, the soft sentimentality of some of his brother Paul Dresser's songs, such as the famed 'On the Banks of the Wabash'] was simply the accumulation of all the facts of his existence... ."

SISTER CARRIE

ESSAY QUESTIONS AND ANSWERS

Question: Discuss the importance of environment in Dreiser's novel.

Answer: Environment seems to be the all-determining factor in the story: it is the universe which buffets man around, instead of vice versa as it is more customary to believe. We see that the deficiencies of Carrie's environment, stage by stage, caused her to wish for and to seek what she had not. Her childhood home was drab and unpromising; she then found her married sister's plodding, resigned existence grim; her dream of success in the Chicago job was soon shattered by the realities of crude, debilitating working conditions. All these blank walls - and others-prod Carrie toward her destiny. Hurstwood likewise was preconditioned for his fate by his glamorous but materially limited managerial position, and by the home atmosphere perpetuated by his selfish, grasping wife and two spoiled children. Environment is thus at the back of each character, pushing him compulsively toward more money, more pleasure, more success-or else, at last, crushing him. It is the key to Dreiser's belief that men are divided into the strong and the weak instead of the good and the bad, and that it is far more common for men to drift in the wind of determinism than to exercise their free will.

Question: Consider as fully as you can the significance of money, and what money will buy, in the novel.

Answer: Money and what it can buy motivates every character in the novel, with the exception of Mr. Ames. Dreiser points this out early in the story (Chapter 7, the beginning), in his important remarks on a "money morality," mentioned earlier. Whereas people, Dreiser believes, have a right to consider the earning of money as a "moral due" and the spending of it as "honestly stored energy," the current notion of money and the spending of it was of "usurped privilege" (a notion probably not confined to the 1900s in America but prevailing to the present day). "Money: something everybody else has and I must get." Carrie's brother-in-law, Hanson, is a necessary Scrooge, and saves pennies. Mrs. Hurstwood calculates how to channel more and more of her husband's earnings into the social success of herself and her children. Drouet gets as much of it as he can because he is one of the "moths," who love pleasure and love to seek out the higher levels of society, just to breathe their affluent atmosphere. For Carrie, as for all the others, money becomes a magnet, drawing her into the paths which, she believes, promise pleasure, success, and happiness. At each stage of her development in the novel, she ultimately rejects those situations which have failed in these results-home, the Hansons, Drouet, Hurstwood. Although gold had always been a god to Hurstwood, too, symbolizing comfort and luxury to which he had become accustomed, he finds after his Chicago fiasco that he is too old, too tired, and too scared to begin the struggle for it again-or is it indeed available to him during his New York **episode**? It is Carrie who learns the most in the novel about the value of material things in her world. She values attractive, fashionable appearance (epitomized to her most, perhaps, by the Broadway parade of people), the "wasteful gastronomy" of the great showplace restaurants of the period (the incident at Sherry's, with the Vances, for example), and her luxurious residence at the Wellington, when she has become a fashionable and successful actress and her name means prestige to the establishment wherein she dwells.

The obverse importance of money is of course hideously depicted by Dreiser, too, in the gradual, downward, tragic path of Hurstwood's life. To trace Hurstwood's financial state from Chicago, to the theft which he partially makes right in Montreal, to the lukewarmly successful bar partnership in New York, to his finding himself with no job and $700 in savings, to the series of 50 cents, 35 cents, 15 cents lodgings of his last days, is to trace his downfall literally. The contrasts throughout between the haves and the have-nots, are richly, grimly painted by Dreiser.

Question: Try to account for Dreiser's realistic, detailed development of either Carrie or Hurstwood in the novel, and tell why they meet the destiny which they do.

Answer: Although one destiny is downward and the other upward, the lives of the two are really parallel results of the deterministic forces of their environments. Dreiser would insist that their inner weaknesses, indecisions, and conflicts are the result of their preconditioning by environment, as well. Thus, to treat Hurstwood's tragedy is to remember what drives Carrie, too-upward, but only into helpless, unhappy material success. Dreiser's point is that it is not the people who are so "wrong," it is the standards of the society in which they find themselves. Hurstwood's story is credible, progresses deliberately, and is memorable. (It goes without saying that Dreiser has devoted some of his most brilliantly descriptive prose to the passages on Hurstwood's - and the New York world's - poverty.) In Chapter

9 we are told, "What he could not correct, he would ignore. There was a tendency in him to walk away from the impossible thing." True, too, of Carrie (or of Drouet), it is likewise true of their natures to be thus drawn easily to the "possible" thing: in Hurstwood's case, Carrie's young charm. But Hurstwood, for all his seeming shrewdness in business, miscalculates in personal relations, and is among the unreflecting characters of the novel. (Ames, again, is the only reflecting character.) "The misfortune of the Hurstwood household was due to the fact that jealousy, having been born of love, did not perish with it," but turned to hate. His wife gathers the forces of hate against him so rapidly with money demands and a pending divorce action, that he is driven to act impulsively, in his so quickly regretted thievery from his employers. From these steps downward it is a process of the New York decline for Hurstwood, where he is but "an inconspicuous drop in an ocean." This is a struggle for a kind of survival which he has not been confronted with before and is not prepared for. His reputation-marring mistake of thievery can never be rectified. Furthermore, Hurstwood is fated to "bad luck" with Carrie in the sense that (1) he deceived her in a number of things, which she discovers but progressively; (2) there was never great love between them-there was mostly his aggressive courting of her - and the relationship thus has no foundation for sympathy and confidence when the going gets rough. In addition, Hurstwood is a pleasure-seeker with the rest, and his bitterness at the deprivation of material things is bound to be all greater by comparison. All these "givens" about the man Hurstwood very credibly preview his eventual apathy-rocking by the radiator and reading the newspaper so that "his difficulties vanished in the items he so well loved to read." They likewise predetermine his tumble into the Bowery flophouses and his commonplace suicide by gas. In any man - but especially in a man like Hurstwood, without foundations of "character" and "reasoning powers" - there is a vital element which dies

when, once secure, confident, and well-placed, he is abruptly jarred and trampled by the world. His self-respect diminishes, his pride is mortally wounded, and his manly spirit fades away. This is what happened to Hurstwood, and each stage of his deterioration paves the way for the subsequent stage.

Question: Give brief consideration to one virtue and one fault of the novel.

Answer: Aside from Dreiser's skillful, even brilliant use of descriptive detail in order to depict social conditions of the 1990s, I would say that his attitude toward his material and his people is worth commenting on. Dreiser does not stand above or superior to his characters; rather he seems understanding and sympathetic, treating them almost tenderly. As Carl Van Doren puts it, "He stood beside them when he told their story." He can sigh over and deplore humanity but he cannot take it upon himself to convict and punish. His attitude is nonjudgmental, nonmoralizing; it is a view related to his philosophy that man is a wisp in the wind, a waif of nature, and that the world is without sufficient reason or meaning to us. It is through his attitude, indeed, that he conveys this deterministic philosophy and focuses on the age-old conflict between instinct and reason, emotion and logic. Man is in a stage of development where he is buffeted between the two forces, never wholly governed by one or the other. Dreiser's whole portrayal of his characters in drifting, dissatisfied, indecisive situations conveys this theory.

An element especially troublesome to the modern reader is Dreiser's habit of telling outright what might be implied or revealed by action. Some examples are: "Her fancy plunged recklessly into privileges and amusements which would have been much more becoming had she been cradled a child of fortune." Or "The poor girl thrilled as she walked away from

Drouet." Or "Sunday passed with equal doubts, worries, assurances, and heaven knows what vagaries of mind and spirit." (The last quoted sentence indicates another element which the reader may consider, according to his own taste, as either quaint or annoying "colloquialism.")

Question: Discuss the treatment of sex in the novel, in an attempt to explain why the novel aroused a storm of protest upon its appearance in 1900.

Answer: Although to the modern reader, accustomed in some cases to blow-by-blow accounts of sexual relations, the question of "sex" in Sister Carrie may seem unemphatic, the reader need only be reminded of the milieu of latter-day Victorian America into which Dreiser's story of a girl who enters into two illicit and prolonged liaisons was dropped, to realize that protest was inevitable. On these relationships of Carrie's the author placidly built the foundation of his novel. It is through her very seeking, yet drifting, indecisive nature, that she first accepts Drouet's financial aid. Drouet is "actuated by a keen desire for the feminine," and is openly depicted as an industrious little "masher." Later it is a question of the sophisticated, polished Hurstwood who does not even hesitate in his deceptions when bent with middle-aged determination on gaining Carrie's affections. It was of little concern to the strictly moral-minded reader of that period that Carrie's drifting into two men's lives without benefit of clergy and with but vague flutterings of conscience was part of the author's larger point about all such human beings. Carrie merely represents them.

Further protest was no doubt aroused by Dreiser's conscientious avoidance of moralizing or judgments. In his universe there is no conventional system of rewards and punishments. By conventional standards, Dreiser even refuses to judge in the end, although it cannot escape the reader that Carrie has found success without happiness, which is the result of a society which genuflected daily to the money god. Readers of yesterday (and perhaps of today?) feel uncomfortable when laws and **conventions** are flouted without conventional punishment following. They also feel uneasy when it is suggested that they have less freedom of will than they would like to imagine. That the author of *Sister Carrie* was making his own compassionate and significant points about people and society may have escaped his first readers.

BIBLIOGRAPHY AND GUIDE TO FURTHER RESEARCH

A detailed listing of all of Theodore Dreiser's works, including the large selection of "primary sources" (manuscripts, letters, clippings, etc.), and further critical and bibliographical references, may be found in F. O. Matthiessen's Theodore Dreiser, *American Men of Letters Series*, New York, 1951. The following references, however, are sufficient to introduce a reader to further research on the various aspects of Dreiser and his work.

Anderson, Sherwood. "Apology for Crudity," *The Dial*, November 8, 1917.

Beach, Joseph Warren. "Realist Fiction; Dreiser," in *The Twentieth Century Novel*, New York, 1932. Representative of that period of Dreiser criticism.

Bourne, Randolph. "The Art of Theodore Dreiser," in *History of a Literary Radical and Other Essays*. New York, 1920.

Chamberlain, John. "Theodore Dreiser," in *After the Genteel Tradition*, ed. Malcolm Cowley. New York, 1936.

Cargill, Oscar. "Naturalists," in *Intellectual America: Ideas on the March*. New York, 1941. A more recent evaluation by an expert on American literature.

Dreiser, Theodore. *An American Tragedy*. New York, 1925.

_____. *Sister Carrie*, with afterword by Willard Thorp. New York, 1961. [original publication, 1900.]

Dudley, Dorothy. *Forgotten Frontiers: Dreiser and the Land of the Free*. New York, 1932. A rather fictionalized biography.

Elias, Robert H. *Theodore Dreiser, Apostle of Nature*. New York, 1949. Detailed but still rather subjective biography.

Farrell, James T. *The Best Short Stories of Theodore Dreiser, introduction*. New York, 1955.

Farrell, James T. *The League of Frightened Philistines*. New York, 1945. Contains lively essays on Dreiser by his admirer.

_____. *Literature and Morality*. New York, 1947.

Freedman, William A. "A Look at Dreiser as Artist: The Motif of Circularity in *Sister Carrie*." *Modern Fiction Studies*, VIII (1963), 384–392. A current evaluation.

Holiday, Billie with William Dufty. *Lady Sings the Blues*. New York, 1965.

Kazin, Alfred. *On Native Grounds*. New York, 1942.

_____. *The Stature of Theodore Dreiser*, ed. Kazin and Charles Shapiro, especially "Theodore Dreiser and His Critics." A useful survey of criticism.

Krutch, Joseph Wood. "Crime and Punishment," *The Nation*, February 20, 1926.

Lehan, Richard. "Dreiser's An American Tragedy: A Critical Study," *College English*, XXV (1963), 187–193. A current evaluation.

Matthiessen, F. O. *Theodore Dreiser, The American Men of Letters Series*. New York, 1951. This is an excellent, comprehensive study of Dreiser covering biographical and critical ground.

Mencken, H. L. *A Book of Prefaces*. New York, 1917. Contains essays of comprehensive and illuminating nature on Dreiser, Mencken's friend, correspondent and literary contemporary.

More, Paul Elmer. "Theodore Dreiser, Philosopher," *The Review*, April 17, 1920. An evaluation typical of the 1920s.

Phillips, William L. "The **Imagery** of Dreiser's Novels." *Publications of the Modern Language Association*, LXXVIII (1963), 572–585.

Rahv, Philip. "The Decline of Naturalism," in Image and Idea, New York, 1949. Simplifies critical issues concerning Dreiser.

Sherman, Stuart P. "The Barbaric Nature of Theodore Dreiser," in *On Contemporary Literature*. New York, 1920. A classic "anti" view of Dreiser in the 1920s. It should be noted, however, that Sherman revised this view in "Mr. Dreiser in Tragic Realism," *The Main Stream*, New York, 1927.

Spiller, Robert E. "Theodore Dreiser," in *Literary History of the United States*. Vol. II, New York, 1948. A more recent evaluation.

Trilling, Lionel. "Reality in America," in *The Liberal Imagination*. New York, 1950. A significant assessment by a very discerning contemporary critic of American literature.

Van Doren, Carl. *The American Novel*. New York, 1921, 1940. Van Doren was instrumental in bringing Dreiser more into academic circles of criticism.

Vivas, Eliseo. "Dreiser, An Inconsistent Mechanist," *International Journal of Ethics*, XLVIII, 1938. An important evaluation from the point of view of a critic who is essentially a philosopher.

Walcutt, Charles C. "The Three Stages of Theodore Dreiser's Naturalism." *Publications of the Modern Language Association*, LV, 1940. A careful, scholarly examination of the development of Dreiser's fiction.

Wilson, William Edward. "*The Titan* and *the Gentleman*." *Antioch Review*, XXIII (1963), 25–34.